VAGUE

Interview with Arnold Schwarzenegger not in this issue. Sorry—Arnold was originally to be standing beside this vehicle in full camouflage army fatigues but could not be found. We rented the Hummer, we rented the field, Arnold didn't show.

features

ABOVE:
Karl Lagerhead's
New Minimalism
look is taking off.

RIGHT:
Karl Lagerhead
has his finger on the
pulse of the fashion
world.

OTHER BOOKS FROM THE SAME TWISTED MIND

VAGUE

A FIREFLY BOOK

Cataloguing in Publication Data
Hagey, Thomas
Vague
ISBN 1-55209-056-6
1. Fashion - Humor. 2. Beauty, Personal - Humor.
3. Vogue - Parodies, imitations, etc. I. Title.

PN6231.F36H33 1997 C818'.5402 C97-930858-5

VAGUE, written by Thomas Hagey, is not licensed by or affiliated in any way with any existing magazine or publication. It is strictly a parody.

Published in Canada by
Firefly Books Ltd.
3680 Victoria Park Avenue
Willowdale, Ontario
Canada M2H 3K1

Published in the U.S. by
Firefly Books (U.S.) Inc.
P.O. Box 1338, Ellicott Station
Buffalo, New York, 14205

Printed and bound in Canada

For Marlene De Boer
whose love, support,
and humor
made all of this
possible.

VAGUE

Created, Written and Produced by

Thomas Hagey

Art Direction & Design
Bob Wilcox

Fashion Photography: **Stan Switalski**, Cambridge, Canada
Product Photography: **Steve Lawrence**, Toronto
Creative Consultant/Editor: **Duncan McKenzie**
Copy Editing: **Dan Liebman**; **Angela Pollak**
Fashion Design: **Susan Dicks**, Toronto; **Brad Balch**, Kitchener, Canada
Photo Shoot Coordination **Stephanie Haynes**; **Abby King**
Art & Illustration: **David Prothero**; **Bruce Herchenrader**; **Michael Caunter**
Sean Dawdy; **Ted Sivell**; **Timm Vera**; **Chris Zakrzewski**
Props: **Boardwalk Optical**; **Rapp Optical**; **John Weber**; **Cambridge Towel**;
Brad Balch, the amazing prop maker; **James Sauder**; **Voll motors**
Production Assistance: **Jim Robinson**, Ignition Design; **TTS promotional apparel**, screen printing;
Ken Hartley, photo retouching; **Kevin Weight**, photo manipulation; **Kelvin Case**, North by Northwest;
Mark Bugdale, The Impact Group; **Susan Schaefer**; **Brian Wiebe**
Hair & Makeup: **Andrea Claire Walmsley**; **Heather Brooks**; **Collin Woods**; **Bilal Zeineddine**;
Laura Szucs; **Eve Hrubik**; **Irene Rockwell**; **Lisa Dennison**; **Kendra Schumacher**; **Tex Lillepool**;
Laurie Weichel; **Icon salon & spa**
Models & Actors: **Tara Sinnett**, cover model; **Mark Bergen**; **Marlene De Boer**; **Rob Nickerson**;
Naomi Blicker; **Jennifer Jacobson**; **Jennifer Faulds**; **Bruce Hunter**; **Katherine Ashby**;
Stephanie Haynes; **Janet Van De Graaff**; **Blair Bender**; **Teresa Pavlinek**; **Stephanie Guest**;
Jude Winterbottom; **Tammy Withrow**; **Lisa Maslanka**; **Jeff Maslanka**; **Heather Eve McKearnan**;
Michael Rouse; **Jennifer Swann**; **Collin Woods**; **Amanda Moir**; **Steven Wong**; **James Hall**;
Richard Sanders (AKA Les Nessman); **Vanessa Tikkala**; **Ross Fraser**; **Lora Zulijani**; **Sage Walmsley**;
Woodruff the Jack Russell by **Hot Pursuit Kennels**; Breeding pigs by the **Crow family**;
Melissa Wanklin; **Belise Abwunza**; **Sarah Cressman**; **Val Kinzie**
Special Thanks: **Richard Sanders**; **Hank Sternberg**; **Reid Bannister**; **Mary E. Lea**; **Donald Lea**;
The Beirnes family; **Kim & Paul McAuley**; **Alex & Vicky Taylor**; **Jim & Ellyn Robinson**;
Martin Meissner; **Abby King**; **Stankiewicz family**; **Lloyd & Bertha Hagey**; **Zwart family**;
Lakeroad Catering; **Media Focus**; **Dan Grady**; **Mark & Phyllis Silverstein** @ **Studio City Guest
House and Spa**; **Mike Melnychuk**; **Ted Giesbrecht**; **Jono Turlej**; **Kent & Cha Heiden**; **Pamela Main**;
Stanley Peter Owens; **Doug Scheerer**; **Tracey Alexander**; **Bruce Ettinger**; **Smith Hart** and everyone at
ICW; **Donald & Nancy Tikkala**; **Helene Couture**; **Janet Verrips**; **Deanna & Carl Gmelin**;
Circo Bar & Grill; **Gord & Judy Rottar**; **Randy Rodriguez**, **Rio Bravo Trading Company**, Santa Fe;
Harry Mathews; **John Whitney**; **Christina & Dave Tomlinson**; **Simpson Lumber**; **John Brunton**;
John Hagey; the **Beckers**; **Wendy Davis**; **Bob & Anke**; **Fernanda Sousa**; **Renée LaLonde**;
Amy McKenzie; **Lionel Koffler**; **Michael Worek**; **Superior Safety**; jet pilots, **Bill Robinson &
Stu Swanson**; **Fliteline Services Ground Crew**; **Bloomingdale Service**; **Dr. & Ms Achtymichuk**
Translation: **Vanessa Stankiewicz**; **Anke Davids**; **Nikka Times**; **Robert J. Ellis**; **Ke Xiang**; **Sean Song**

people are raving about

theater

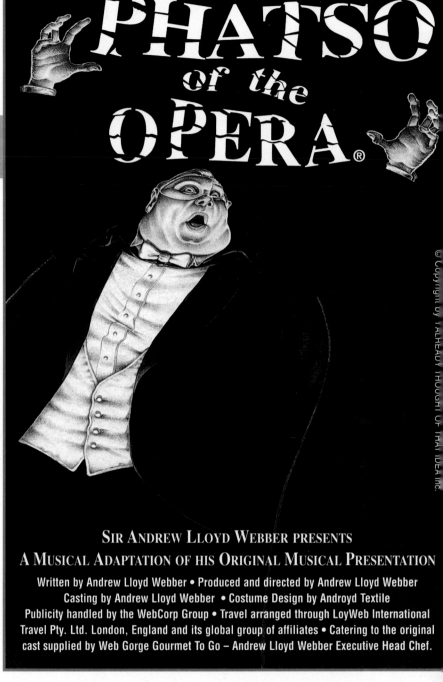

SIR ANDREW LLOYD WEBBER PRESENTS
A MUSICAL ADAPTATION OF HIS ORIGINAL MUSICAL PRESENTATION

Written by Andrew Lloyd Webber • Produced and directed by Andrew Lloyd Webber
Casting by Andrew Lloyd Webber • Costume Design by Androyd Textile
Publicity handled by the WebCorp Group • Travel arranged through LoyWeb International
Travel Pty. Ltd. London, England and its global group of affiliates • Catering to the original
cast supplied by Web Gorge Gourmet To Go – Andrew Lloyd Webber Executive Head Chef

ANDREW LLOYD WEBBER STUBS HIS BIG PHAT TOE

The opening of *Phatso Of The Opera* in London, England, has been tagged as Andrew Lloyd Webber's leap into the icy waters of political incorrectness. There was no shortage of drama as a packed house of loyal followers, dignitaries and media bigwigs witnessed the royal embarrassment. Lloyd Webber's condition is extremely unstable but not life threatening. He has been taken off the critical list and is reported to be recovering in hospital after a severely bruised ego caused him to collapse into the horn section of the orchestra, accidentally killing a musician. The trumpet player, whose name has not been released, died instantly when Lloyd Webber's enormous but delicate ego struck him on the temple.

The incident has left his fans numbed, his critics smacking their lips, and friends as well as hangers-on asking: "Andrew Lloyd Who?"

Lloyd Webber was never one to follow the crowd. But his decision to produce *Phatso* has cast a mammoth hulk of a shadow on his past success and places his entire future in jeopardy.

He could have named it *The Masked Rotundly Challenged Chap of the Opera*, but he chose not to. That would be too safe. As a result, on opening night, Fate's black chauffeur driven limousine quietly idled in the alleyway out back of the theater, patiently awaiting the rising of the curtain and the arrival of the next casualty. Fate, it seems, has all the time in the world. Ironically, the musical began with a fat lady singing. Need I say more? A short while later, much to Sir Andrew Lloyd's dislike, people began walking out of the show. In fact, it became so unpopular, people bought tickets just so they could walk out on it.

We're all tired of political correctness, but do we all go out and make a huge stage production out of it and jam it down the theater-going public's throats? No... (pause), we do not!

Was he hoping to fail? Is he tired of the Midas touch? Was *Phatso* self-sabotage? If not, why would a man of his class take such a creative risk at this point in his career?

Unfortunately we won't have any answers until they take the tubes out of his nose, and while they're at it, his big feet out of his mouth. VAGUE can only assume that Lloyd Webber had tired of political correctness and decided to say it like it is. A big mistake. Everyone hated it, with the exception of the Japanese media. They hailed it as charming, a huge success and a work of genius, but one should expect this brand of optimism from the nation which brought the world Sumo Wrestling.

The public has a difficult enough time dealing with the issue of fat without making matters worse. What possessed him to take such a delicate subject and set it to music? We may never know the answer.

Plans to launch two more politically incorrect productions based on other Andrew Lloyd Webber creations have been halted, at least for now. *Fat Cats* and *Sunset Bowl O'Lard* are temporarily in limbo until options regarding their marketing can be assessed. Judging by the public outrage aimed at *Phatso of the Opera* I would hazard a guess there is an Operatic Fat Lady somewhere at this very moment practicing her scales, waiting for opening night.

While the world sleeps, we are applying the finishing touches to another issue of *VAGUE*. It has been a month of fashion moments.

Yves St. La Croix sends us another one of his scanty lingerie items hot off the plane from Paris. Five of our body perfect editors fight tooth and nail to be the first to try it on. The blood-soaked winner parades about our offices announcing in a monotone voice: "I'm the most beautiful woman in the world, and *this* is my story!"

Armando Armani (loose translation: "Your money or your life") also sends us his absolute best. There's no outfit... no large box of lingerie... no warning... just a postage-due "Greetings from Milan" postcard with a spontaneous doodle on the back. So perfect. So well chosen. So... Armani! We can only wonder how he finds the time to design amid his hectic letter-writing agenda.

The flurry of activity here at *VAGUE* can only mean one thing: "Once again" fashion is on the move. "Once again" designers are emerging from gout treatment clinics; "once again" they have sworn off anything in a heavy cream sauce. But why? When are these male designers going to realize that "tossing your cookies" is no longer reserved for those gloriously trim, emaciated models. It was good enough for Roman centurions; it's surely good enough for overweight designers.

But enough about the industry's jagged little pill. Let's retire gorge and purge to the back burner and get on with the business of fashion. It's a challenge to reinvent the wheel season after season. If you intend to stay on top you can't rest on your laurels or you risk becoming "a fat ass." "Once again" the designers are promising to deliver quality and originality at a price which will allow them to cover their overheads comfortably.

TOP RIGHT: JEAN CLAUDE CLOD'S NOW-FAMOUS LETTUCE HAT

BOTTOM LEFT: CEO/DESIGNER HARRY KRISHNA IS THE NEW CAT'S ASS OF THE FASHION WORLD

RIGHT: SOME WOMAN WHO WANDERED INTO MY OFFICE ONE DAY CLAIMING TO BE A MAN TRAPPED IN A WOMAN'S CLOTHES

With the recession now officially over, it is "once again" okay to appear rich. Frugality is still in, but now it's expensive. "Once again" we encourage you to cough up the big bucks; it's what separates the Lady of the house from the hired help.

This month **Umberto Garbaggio** reinvents the bag lady with his recycled fabrics collection, **Krishna Dior** continues his climb to prominence as his divine fashion consciousness catches fire, and **Jean Claude Clod** redefines *Hat Couture,* proving "once again" that it's not what's inside your head that counts.

All things considered, it should be an exciting issue. At this point we ask that you sit back, relax, enjoy the trip; we should be landing in Paris shortly. Have a great day and remember that although there's nothing wrong with looking fabulous, fashion *has* been described as the subtle art of self-deception. Self-deception: the ingenious ability of pulling the wool over your own eyes.

Anna Whirlwintour

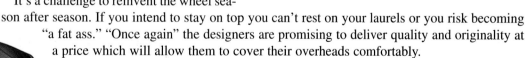

Vague trends

by contributing writer
Lance Boyle

The Zit is a Hit!

THE SIMPLE PIMPLE SQUEEZES ITS WAY INTO THE LIMELIGHT

Over the centuries the mole has been admired as a symbol of beauty. Some of the most idolized women in the world have had moles: Marilyn Monroe, Elizabeth Taylor, Madonna and Cindy Crawford. What was it that launched these glamorous careers? A great body? Talent? Or a brown blemish with the hair in the middle?

Yes, it was the mole which twisted the rubbery arm of popularity in their favor.

For years the mole has been the blot of beauty, the queen of the molehill, numero uno. But is it on the verge of being replaced? Now a new contender threatens to burrow away at the mole's sex appeal and alluring grip on the fashion-conscious public. We refer, of course, to the pimple.

In this issue of *VAGUE* we take a look behind the zit phenomenon that has taken the world by storm. We learn to say Au revoir MOLE and Bonjour ZIT.

The Unusual Becomes Beautiful

It may have taken the world by surprise, but there is nothing unusual about the zit's popularity and rapid rise to prominence. Like POISON perfume before it, the negative image surrounding the zit has done nothing to limit its appeal. Quite the opposite—the threat, the daring stigma, the taboo of the zit is an essential part of its fascination. Starting out as a barely noticeable blip on the lip of fashion this pustule outcast has grown and risen, until its popularity has reached the point of exploding.

A New "Pop" Icon—
What's the Fuss About Pus?

The arrival of the pimple on the world stage has left beauty experts miffed, cosmetic and chemaceutical company executives worried and supermodels scrambling to grow their own, get bacterial implants or pack their clothes and go home.

Could anyone have foreseen such a turnabout? A few short months ago it was every young woman's nightmare. A condition which added more anxiety to the pre-prom night jitters than the anticipation of losing one's virginity to some fumbling, insensitive, adolescent guy. Yet the zit has become all the rage. No matter where you go—clubs, cafés, the opera—the zit is not only on everyone's lips but on their chins, foreheads and cheeks as well.

No longer is the zit youth's fashion statement. Its popularity bulges through barriers of age, race and financial status. Beauty watchers claim you can tell a person's true wealth by the way they carry their zits. People of "old money" display them discreetly around the neckline or beside the ear, one more thing comfortably within their grasp. Whereas the nouveau riche tend to flaunt their newfound wealth by squeezing them in public.

The Zit Is Here To Stay

Like false eyelashes and fake fingernails, it looks like the zit will be around for quite some time. If you're squeamish brace yourself. You will wear one eventually. You will stand in line with everyone else to get that doozy of an oozy.

Battle Against Zit Comes To Head

Not everyone is embracing the trend. The manufacturers of acne-fighting formulas have watched in horror as profits plunged to all-time lows. Says one executive, "We're literally getting squeezed out of the market." Many of these companies have collectively injected advertising dollars toward a media blitz to convince the public that the trend is goofy and potentially dangerous. The campaign is not considered a lost gauze as yet, but early indications reveal they aren't soaking up much support with it either.

Juicy Profits In Zit Accessories

Zitco, manufacturers of *The Zit Kit*, and their competition *Acme Acne Inc.*, makers of *Squeeze Me, I'm Yours,* are the first two companies out on the market with implants and stick-ons. Both have reported landslide profits and are extremely optimistic about their future in fostering festering, but neither has forgotten what happened to the now defunct Dow Corning Company, the breast implant giant that sought bankruptcy protection when their hooters came home to roost.

Still, so far (touch silicone) everyone is very pleased with their zit implants, but trends change. There are no guarantees to manufacturers that recipients won't sue. As long as the courts keep awarding huge settlements, legal battles will continue to flare up and run rampant.

The Zit Kit, manufactured by Zitco, is sweeping the globe. These stick-on accessories offer fashion-conscious consumers the instant zit look. ($59)

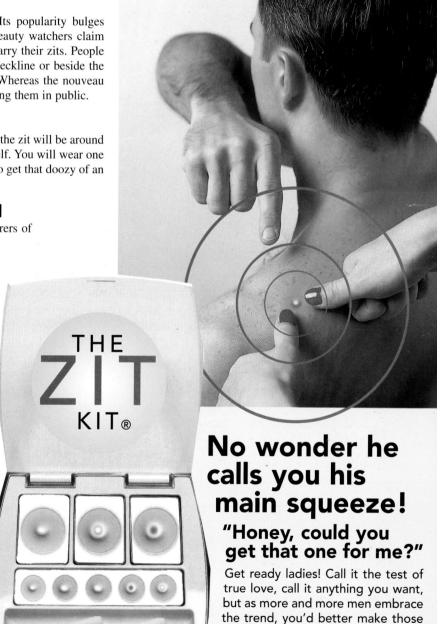

No wonder he calls you his main squeeze!

"Honey, could you get that one for me?"

Get ready ladies! Call it the test of true love, call it anything you want, but as more and more men embrace the trend, you'd better make those thumb nails available.

Vague books

Sunny Rhodes breaks new ground in the "How To" book genre, with the landmark release of *The Merry Widow*. This step-by-step guide is a must-read for any woman who has patiently, patiently, run out of patience.

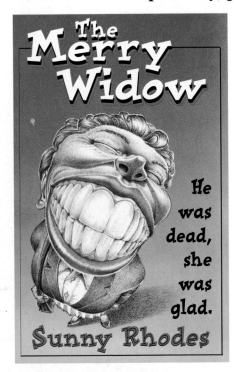

The Merry Widow:
He was dead, she was glad.

By Sunny Rhodes

They say happiness doesn't happen by accident. The Merry Widow is the exception to the rule. Mr. Never-Been-Wrong isn't coming home for dinner anymore and somebody in the house is very glad.

This moving book is one woman's testimony on how to achieve happiness through accidental expiration. The struggle for independence, which leads her to a course in auto mechanics and brake line maintenance. A course from which she would eventually earn an "A" plus. An "A" plus which would lead to that lonely, slippery stretch of highway known as Devil's Bend. As for her husband, it's too bad Todd isn't here to join in the fun, but "them's the brakes!" Female determination and a great deal of insurance have paved the way to a much merrier future for the author.

$22.95 Hardcorpse, Graves & Jyvanaditch Publishers N.Y. N.Y.

Beyond The Fridge:
Food For Thought

by Candice B. Wolfed

The diet book that takes you out of the kitchen, out of the house, onto the streets and into the exciting new world of possibilities.

Ahh! the beckoning fridge. Many a woman's battle with low self-esteem begins here. Take control of your life. Learn to resist the "Snack Attack."

Over 100 pages of Calorie-reduced advice and Fat-free alternatives which will ultimately lead to a happier you. This book demonstrates how to recognize the fine line between "Having A Wee Bite To Eat" and "Slamming The Groceries Into You!" It hammers home the message that although supermarkets have hundreds of items, they don't all have to end up back at your place. Remember, they have other customers too.

$24.95 Simon & Shister, The Self Help Specialists

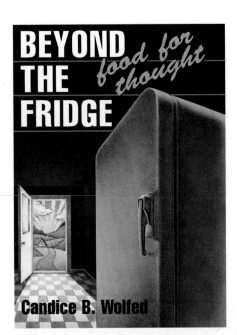

Cross Dogs And
Over Anxious Women

by Lyle Lyttle

"There was a time when a woman never took her man to the cleaners unless his suit actually needed pressing."

At last! The riveting history of the feminist movement written from a man's perspective. A lightly spirited chronicling of the fight not only for equality, but for the unfair advantage women now enjoy in a world once dominated by men.

You will relive the helpless male years when men didn't vacuum, didn't babysit, didn't watch their backs during PMS—but simply stood there and took it like a man. You'll visit a time when men refused to cook or pick up the kids from day care, or bear their souls, or exercise their feminine side because they'd be called "wimp."

Yes, thanks to the movement many men are now champions and serious rivals in a world of worthy domestic chores once dominated by women. They are still, however, accused of being wimps, but they are secure in the knowledge that the feminist movement was partly about the liberation of men; and for this they have the stronger sex to thank—women, of course!

Hardcover $29.95 Rangdom House Publishers New York New York

ATURITY

FOR MEN

Men and maturity?

Sounds like a
contradiction in terms...
until now.

MATURITY
from Calvin Kline

MATURITY
FOR MEN

eau de toilette

His Art Hangs in the White House
But His Latest Work Has Been Created Just for You.

The Lady with the Ball and Chain

(also known as "Our Lady of Perpetual Crankiness") is now available in snow-white porcelain from who else but The Frankly Mint.

The art of Gianini Porcelini is in museums and priceless collections around the world. His newest masterpiece promises not only to enhance the elegance of your home but will alert members of the opposite sex that there is, indeed, a lady in the house. And for about a week out of every month, they may well be living on borrowed time. Tweaked your interest yet? There's more!

Inspired by the blue and white porcelain of Josiah Wedgwood over 200 years ago, this marble-like porcelain will be treasured for its depth, width, height and delicate detail. Not to mention the thrill of partial nakedness.

This enchanting cameo captures the legend of "That Special Time" (often, for good reasons, referred to as The Wrong Time) and achieves this like no other work of art. It is splendidly matted in linen and framed in solid realistic wood, ready to display.

Frankly, it's only available from The Frankly Mint. And quite frankly, if you don't place your order quickly, this limited edition will be sold out. This specially imported work is priced at only $295—very reasonable for handcrafted porcelain art by an internationally renowned artist, spotlighting a subject as delicate as this one. Frankly, we've never before seen quality of this caliber at such an affordable price.

His previous works pertaining to women's issues, most notably *Guilt* & *Laundry,* sold out in less than a month. Don't be disappointed. Reserve NOW!!!

The Lady with the Ball and Chain

The burden of menstruation
NOW IN SNOW-WHITE PORCELAIN

RESERVATION APPLICATION

Please enter my order for "The Lady With The Ball And Chain," an original work of art by Gianini Porcelini (the guy we've never heard of before, but apparently he's famous). I understand that no payment is necessary at this time. Please also bill me later for the amusingly small deposit of $59 when the work is ready to be sent to me, and for the balance in four equal "monthly installments" of $59 each. I understand that these things are most likely stacked in your warehouse even as we speak and this "waiting period" is just a clever ploy to make us feel that it's worth more than it really is.

The Frankly Mint®, Frankly Center, Washington D.C.

SIGNATURE _____
Lawyers and doctors please print.
This is merely an application, not a
Personal Injury Suit or Prescription Form.

NAME _____

ADDRESS _____

CITY _____

STATE/ZIP _____

The Frankly Mint... *We put stuff in your house.*®

Vague movies

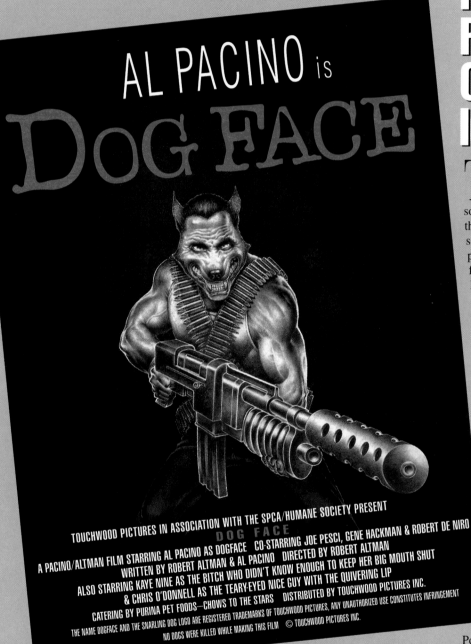

AL PACINO is
DOG FACE

TOUCHWOOD PICTURES IN ASSOCIATION WITH THE SPCA/HUMANE SOCIETY PRESENT
DOG FACE
A PACINO/ALTMAN FILM STARRING AL PACINO AS DOGFACE   CO-STARRING JOE PESCI, GENE HACKMAN & ROBERT DE NIRO
WRITTEN BY ROBERT ALTMAN & AL PACINO   DIRECTED BY ROBERT ALTMAN
ALSO STARRING KAYE NINE AS THE BITCH WHO DIDN'T KNOW ENOUGH TO KEEP HER BIG MOUTH SHUT
& CHRIS O'DONNELL AS THE TEARY-EYED NICE GUY WITH THE QUIVERING LIP
CATERING BY PURINA PET FOODS—CHOWS TO THE STARS   DISTRIBUTED BY TOUCHWOOD PICTURES INC.
THE NAME DOGFACE AND THE SNARLING DOG LOGO ARE REGISTERED TRADEMARKS OF TOUCHWOOD PICTURES. ANY UNAUTHORIZED USE CONSTITUTES INFRINGEMENT
NO DOGS WERE KILLED WHILE MAKING THIS FILM   © TOUCHWOOD PICTURES INC.

Is Hollywood Running Out Of Original Ideas?

The public is being served up remakes, something-likes, sequels and rehashes to the point of nausea. Not only do the titles sound identical but the story lines are suspiciously familiar as well. It's a formula for success which doesn't necessarily have anything to do with great entertainment—and an illness that you shouldn't expect to disappear just yet.

Dog Face, the latest release from Touch Wood Pictures Inc, starring Al Pacino, does not fall into the retread, tediously thin on substance category. This vaguely familiar cross between two of Pacino's earlier hits, *Scarface* and *Dog Day Afternoon,* is both powerful and riveting. American movie critics Sisko & Egbert loved it so much they gave it the first-ever *four thumbs up* rating.

Pacino works his magic as Dog Face. There's biting suspense, and the action never stops.

Touch Wood Pictures keeps walking the tightrope as rumors of another Pacino-cast canine theme film is currently in development. *Scent of a Dog* is to commence shooting next June, followed next spring by *Dogfather—Life's a Bitch in the Mafia...* Are they longshots? Possibly, but if anyone can pull it off it'll be Al Pacino.

Dog Face
Touch Wood Pictures Inc.
Al Pacino is back and he's off to South America to kick the drug lords' asses. Only this time he has a bit of a supernatural surprise in store for them. Killer suspense leaves the audience howling, snarling and begging for more.

"Pacino is powerful, riveting, larger than life! We haven't seen such a thriller since the release of *Bad Girl's Dormitory*. Non-stop crescendo of action, suspense and Milk-Boners—**A big Four Thumbs Up**"
–Sisko & Egbert, movie critics to the world

15

MORE
Vague movies

Waterworld II– The Last Bath

It floated into the theaters this month but failed to take the public by storm. It's the non-awaited sequel to Waterworld. Judging by the box office receipts, the only people who were really impatiently awaiting it were the investors of Waterworld I. They already paid for the horrendously expensive set and the axed action footage from the original movie, so why not attempt to retrieve some of that $200 million budget?

Sisko & Egbert Introduce Four Thumbs Up Rating

HOLLYWOOD – When somebody talks about putting four thumbs up, I immediately ask where? and whose? I fear with all these loose references to thumbs that the word *swiveling* is not too far away, and I don't like it one little bit.

Recently Sisko & Egbert—movie critics to the world—released news of their Four Thumbs Up film rating. Hopefully it means that Hollywood will be delivering more for the moviegoer's dollar. Don't hold your breath. It won't be long before the public discovers that four thumbs up is really just two thumbs up with two extra thumbs thrown in to keep pace with inflation.

> "Gone is the recycled urine-drinking scene in the first minute of the film. Aside from that, it's the same old same old..."

KEVIN COSTNER
WATERWORLD II
THE LAST BATH

UNIVERSAL PICTURES AND WISH UPON A STAR ENTERTAINMENT CONSORTIUM PRESENT
WATERWORLD II – THE LAST BATH
STARRING KEVIN (JUST READ THE CONTRACT!) COSTNER   ALSO STARRING DENNIS HOPPER AS THE MAN WHO WOULDN'T DIE
MUSIC BY: OBVIOUSLY SOMEONE KEVIN PICKED   DIRECTED INDIRECTLY BY KEVIN COSTNER/GUN TO THEIR HEADS PRODUCTIONS
SOUND BY DOLBY   MR. COSTNER'S PADDLE BOAT BY BUD'S BUDGET AQUATIC VEHICLES
WHISKEY BY JACK DANIELS   CIGARETTES COMPLIMENTS OF R.J. REYNOLDS
DISTRIBUTED TO SOME EXTENT BY UNIVERSAL PICTURES INC. © UNIVERSAL PICTURES INC.

Waterworld II – The Last Bath
Universal Pictures

Gone is the recycled urine-drinking scene in the first minute of the film. Dennis Hopper makes an amazing return from hell... And Kevin Costner is definitely one strange kinda guy. Why would a young and virile male—for the second time— choose drifting around on a boat in an ocean of indifference when he has a chance to live out a fantasy with a beautiful woman on an island with an endless supply of Jack Daniels whiskey?... It may take one more sequel for the investors to get their money back.

For Work Or Foreplay

EVEN MORE
Vague movies
THE SEQUELS CONTINUE

So just how does Hollywood come up with all those boffo movie titles, anyway? With idea reserves running increasingly low, many are using computers to generate new titles automatically from existing titles. Check out where the industry is heading with some of these possible remakes and future smash hit sequels!

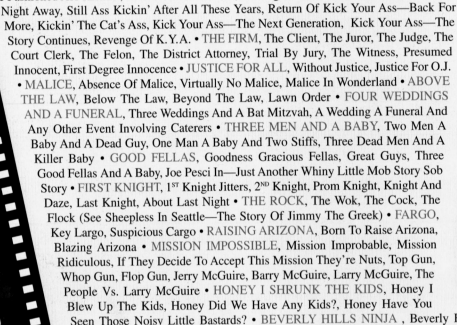

DIE HARD, Die Harder, Do or Die Even Harder, Die Hardest, Live And Let Die Hard • SLEEPING WITH THE ENEMY, Sleeping Through An Enema, Sleeping With The Nanny • SLEEPLESS IN SEATTLE, Sleeveless In Seattle, Sheepless In Seattle—The Story Of Jimmy The Greek • JEAN-CLAUDE VANN DAMME In: Kick Your Ass 1, Kick Your Ass 2, Kick My Ass Or I'll Kick Yours, Good Olde Fashioned Ass Kickin', Son Of Kick Your Ass, Waiting To Kick Your Ass, Ass Kickin' The Night Away, Still Ass Kickin' After All These Years, Return Of Kick Your Ass—Back For More, Kickin' The Cat's Ass, Kick Your Ass—The Next Generation, Kick Your Ass—The Story Continues, Revenge Of K.Y.A. • THE FIRM, The Client, The Juror, The Judge, The Court Clerk, The Felon, The District Attorney, Trial By Jury, The Witness, Presumed Innocent, First Degree Innocence • JUSTICE FOR ALL, Without Justice, Justice For O.J. • MALICE, Absence Of Malice, Virtually No Malice, Malice In Wonderland • ABOVE THE LAW, Below The Law, Beyond The Law, Lawn Order • FOUR WEDDINGS AND A FUNERAL, Three Weddings And A Bat Mitzvah, A Wedding A Funeral And Any Other Event Involving Caterers • THREE MEN AND A BABY, Two Men A Baby And A Dead Guy, One Man A Baby And Two Stiffs, Three Dead Men And A Killer Baby • GOOD FELLAS, Goodness Gracious Fellas, Great Guys, Three Good Fellas And A Baby, Joe Pesci In—Just Another Whiny Little Mob Story Sob Story • FIRST KNIGHT, 1ST Knight Jitters, 2ND Knight, Prom Knight, Knight And Daze, Last Knight, About Last Night • THE ROCK, The Wok, The Cock, The Flock (See Sheepless In Seattle—The Story Of Jimmy The Greek) • FARGO, Key Largo, Suspicious Cargo • RAISING ARIZONA, Born To Raise Arizona, Blazing Arizona • MISSION IMPOSSIBLE, Mission Improbable, Mission Ridiculous, If They Decide To Accept This Mission They're Nuts, Top Gun, Whop Gun, Flop Gun, Jerry McGuire, Barry McGuire, Larry McGuire, The People Vs. Larry McGuire • HONEY I SHRUNK THE KIDS, Honey I Blew Up The Kids, Honey Did We Have Any Kids?, Honey Have You Seen Those Noisy Little Bastards? • BEVERLY HILLS NINJA , Beverly Hills Cop 1, 2 & 3, Little Beverly Hills Snot • BRAD PITT in: Legends Of The Fall, The Legend Of Those Fools • SCARFACE, Cigar Face, Bizarre Face, Guitar Face • GUILTY BY SUSPICION, Beyond Suspicion, Above Suspicion, We're Not Suspicious And We Don't Give A Shit If He's Guilty Either • BOILING POINT, Vanishing Point, What's Your Point?, Don't Point! • PRIMAL RAGE, Primal Fear, Primal Instinct, Primal Horniness, Primal Time Television • STEVEN SEGAL in: Under Siege, Under Sarge—Steven Segal Meets Sgt. Bilko, On Dangerous Ground, On Bumpy Terrain, Hard To Kill • SCHINDLER'S LIST, Schindler's Other List, Schindler's Christmas Wish List, Schindler's Lips, Schindler's Lisp • JUST CAUSE, Just Because—And Don't Ask So Many Bloody Questions • MURDER BY DEATH, Murder For No Apparent Reason, Murder In The 1ST, 2ND & 3RD, Murder By Intercourse—The Trial Of Johnny The Schlong, Murder By Dangerous Indiscretion, Murder By Proxy, Murder Because Of Primal Rage With Extreme Prejudice And Without Just Cause • SENSE AND SENSIBILITY, Senseless But I Sense Stability, Incest And Sensitivity • FREE WILLY, Free Willy Too, Free Your Wet Willie, Free Willie Winkie, Either Lock It Up Or Let The Damn Fish Go Free—One Or The Other!!!

Shop Till You Drop!

Our Customers Come Last.

At American Excess, our customers come last. But, when it comes to shopping, any fool knows whoever finishes last wins.

You too can win big if you shop with the American Excess Platinum® card. It gets you what you want—

even what you don't need—faster than any card we know of. And with no pre-set spending limit, your legs will give out before your credit does.

So, "shop till you drop" and experience the amazing difference that Platinum makes.

®

American Excess... membership has its casualties.®

Youthful skin is just the beginning.

Is your cleansing puff
trying to tell you something?

OIL
of
OLD LADY

A breakthrough? You bet it is!

Scientists at OIL OF OLD LADY have made an exciting discovery. They've uncovered a rich oil in mature women which combats the aging process. We believe it achieves this in much the same way that the venom of poisonous snakes acts as an antidote for victims of snake bites. When used as directed, Oil Of Old Lady gently turns back the hands of time, producing results which stop at nothing short of remarkable. It's so effective in the prevention of lines and wrinkles that, by comparison, it makes Retin-A and Alpha Hydroxy Acids seem like… well, 'Snake Oil.' It actually reverses the process of aging, leaving your skin firm, smooth and supple—like no other product in the history of the world. All this in a shower scrub! And, when administered as intended, it not only eliminates odors, but delivers youthful-looking skin almost overnight.

Which brings us to the moral question...

We'd like to dismiss the rumors and innuendo flying around about kidnaping the elderly, missing persons and ritual grindings. In their selfish undying pursuit of fortune and publicity, it appears that our competitors will stop at nothing to maintain their own unfair share of the market. These allegations of unethical conduct are not only damaging and unfounded... they're really starting to annoy us. So, once and for all for the record, "We have done nothing WRONG!"

However, if you know of a loved one who would like to further the cause of scientific discovery, please don't hesitate to sign the donor card on the back of that special someone's driver's license. Then call this toll-free number for more information about our no-obligation money-making opportunity.

Phone: 1-800-SELL-GRANNY.
No detailed questions asked.
No further correspondence.
Offer void where prohibited
(but we're negotiating with politicians).

We've discovered the secret to youthful-looking skin
...and what to do about granny ®

Where toilet water really

France's *Eau de toilette* region still a mystery to most.

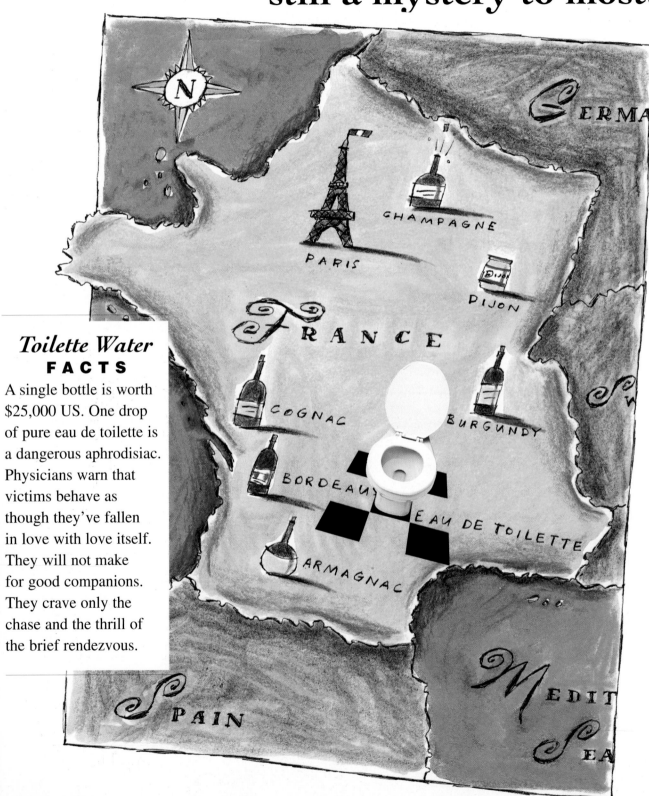

Toilette Water
FACTS

A single bottle is worth $25,000 US. One drop of pure eau de toilette is a dangerous aphrodisiac. Physicians warn that victims behave as though they've fallen in love with love itself. They will not make for good companions. They crave only the chase and the thrill of the brief rendezvous.

comes from.

Perhaps you consider yourself a connoisseur of the finer things in life? Can you *hold your own* against the best? VAGUE bets that when it comes to the origin of toilet water, even the most cultured individual will discover they're still a little wet behind the ears.

There is a place in France where the water trickles forth by its own free will, appears out of practically nowhere with only a little help from humans. Hand ladled with great care by peasant workers who know why they're there. They are not in any great rush; they can't be. They must wait and be patient with the understanding that you cannot prod the will of nature with the same stick that you discipline the obstinate swine. The region of which I speak is known to those of good breeding as *EAU DE TOILETTE*

Close to some of the most famous wine regions in the world there is a region unlike any other, where a very special industry quietly *goes* about its *business* practically unnoticed. Yet each year they do more than a billion dollars' worth of business in a world market which they alone dominate.

When it comes to the originality of liquids the French are fiercely territorial. If you produce bubbly you better not call it champagne unless it actually comes from the region of Champagne. So why would one expect it to be any different when it comes to toilet water? If it doesn't say eau de toilette on the label, it may not even come from toilets, and it definitely doesn't come from the region of Eau de toilette.

Long before Jean-Luc de Bastarde popularized toilet water, the custom of putting something sweet-smelling behind the ears was introduced by the French. Since that time it has become almost as popular as the annoying practice of double mock kissing on both sides of the face (Mmmwha! Mmmwha! Mmmwha! Mmmwha!). Both are examples of "Pretense de la France" and have spread throughout the civilized world.

Pure toilet water is older than the toilet itself. Gathered from the bowl at the peak of perfection, it's trod on by tender loving feet to enhance and release precious character traits.Then it's immediately plunged into wooden casks so that the air cannot get at it, and aged in oxygen-free storage for two years.

"Wine maketh glad
zee heart of man,
but zee toilet wataire,
she is seemply grande."

—Jean-Luc de Bastarde

"If it doesn't say Eau de toilette on the label, it doesn't come from toilets."

When the waiting is over, the casks are brought out into the sunlight for the filtering off of the salty sediment. It is a special day, a celebration of the bounty of the bowl. The priest is presented with the first bottle, and after it has been blessed the bell in the church steeple rings and continues to do so until the last bottle has been corked and sealed with a washer and lock-nut. Everyone marvels at the clarity.

At long last, it is ready to be shipped to the toilet water manufacturers. The doings are done but the work is not over. It must begin again as it always has in the tiny region known as Eau de toilette. They are a simple people with a singular purpose, living out their lives the only way they know how.

FROM
KARL
It's the

I DON'T HAVE A THING TO WEAR!

FRESH FROM THE SHOWER
COLLECTION

Oh yes you do.
What could be simpler?
You emerge from the
shower and while
still dripping wet
wrap yourself in a towel
and off you go to the
airport onto a private jet,
destination unknown.
It's free, bold, radical,
fluffy, absorbent,
unconventional styling
—it's the least you can do.

new minimalism
LAGERHEAD
least you can do

The Divine House of Krishna Dior

Remember us? We used to annoy you in airports!

Harry Krishna, CEO and head designer, is wearing Krishna Dior's
i AM NOT THIS SHIRT t-shirt ($90)
Saffron-orange pants ($120)
Kama Sutra jacket ($650)
sports sunglasses ($85)
designer forehead dot ($8.50)

In the beginning, God created *Christian Dior*. Then, out of the blue another religion picked up on the successful Dior name and built an empire based on one simple question, "Do you have any spare change?"

Times have changed since the early days, and Krishna Dior's marketing focus is no longer restricted to hitting up the traveling public for loose change before they board a jetliner. In fact, Krishna execs now board airliners of their own as they run a door-to-door network that matches those of Avon and Mary Kay. In addition, they own and operate legitimate boutiques in airports, shopping malls and upscale chain stores worldwide.

Financial experts scratch their heads, wondering how a bunch of passive street corner panhandlers ended up with a five hundred million dollar empire without involving backers or incurring a bank loan. Such skepticism amuses company CEO and head designer Harry Krishna.

"The answer is simple," he says with a smile. "We may look funny, but we understand an important aspect of human behavior. We observed that, first, if you are annoying, people will tell you to go away. Second, if you are annoying *enough*, people will *pay* you to go away. We based our business plan on the second scenario."

Ramma Ramma Ding Dong Move Over Avon Here Comes Krishna Dior

Krishna Dior embarked on a business venture which created a new fashion giant. The company's first initiative was to develop Dior to Door® sales. The approach went like so: Polite sales people wearing orange pants arrive at the door with their merchandise. The occupant of the home is presented with an attractive catalog. While the customer browses, the salesperson showers them with love, does a little dance, chants a few songs and writes up the order—all in a low pressure environment. Three days later they return with the goods and the transaction is complete. True, it's a bit of a song and dance routine, but the experience is so weird that people are falling in love with the saffron disciples of divine design.

It's a far cry from asking for handouts on street corners in exchange for that massive impossible-to-comprehend volume on eastern religion (which does, by the way, make for a delightful doorstop).

> **"If** you are reincarnated as *Bullwinkle the Moose*—and obviously you're not a size 8 anymore—Krishna Dior's GUARANTEED FOR LIFE AFTER LIFE REFUND POLICY allows you to return the outfit any time in the future—no questions asked. This makes Krishna Dior the first design house in fashion history to not only stand behind their products but in front of them as well. **"**

The Karma Lottery ®

But, the most unusual aspect of Krishna Dior's sales strategy is surely the Karma Lottery Scratch 'n' Win ticket—one comes free with every purchase. Those lucky enough to hold a winning ticket receive *Good Karma Points* —anywhere from 10 (don't laugh—it's the difference between coming back as a squid or a dog) to 40,000 (which guarantees demigod status after death, along with dinner for two at the Krishna Curry Palace).

Says Harry Krishna: "Everyone is willing to pack reincarnation away somewhere in the back of their mind. It's unnerving enough concentrating on *this* life without worrying about what you may be faced with in the next as a result of shortsightedness. How many little people—or even cockroaches—are we safely allowed to squash in this life without seriously inconveniencing ourselves on the next plane of existence through bad karma? Will I be moving forward or back? Should I invest in stocks or treasury bills? These are the questions we must all ask ourselves."

Such disarming honesty is typical of the man—and he has made sure it is reflected in his company's sales policy.

"When people are out shopping, store employees will tell them that an outfit is *becoming* just so the salesperson can make the sale... 'Oh, it's YOU! It's definitely YOU!' I do not believe in this approach. It's not what's on the outside that counts. Clothes do not really *become* you unless one is inclined not to do laundry; then you have a problem."

His styles are about reliability and overall comfort. They assault and confuse the eye, brilliantly breaking every rule in the book. "My designer t-shirts are printed with the words 'I am not this shirt,'" says Krishna. It is a subtle reminder that the clothes do not make the man or the woman.

Is Krishna saying that clothes are merely useless outer layers? He nods. "Clothes are only essential in that we, in the civilized world, are required to wear them by law. In the larger picture nothing is essential except knowledge through a spiritual existence. We teach our customers that the clothes we sell are, in reality, illusions, practically worthless. We also point out that the wads of cash they hold are also worthless. So why not swap a worthless $2,500 for our worthless attractive silk robe with matching accessories?"

But nowhere is Krishna Dior's integrity more evident than in their approach to sex. "Most of our competitors use sex to sell. They spout off slogans like, "Buy our stuff and get laid." This is an empty promise. I prefer to concentrate on our one simple promise: 'Guaranteed for life... after life... after life...' Our clothes follow you to the next level of existence. If you are reincarnated as Bullwinkle the Moose and the outfit doesn't fit anymore— we'll give you your money back. Although, quite frankly, if you spring for our top-of-the-line Kama Sutra Suit you'll be like heaven to touch—more likely to come back as a mink. Then you'll get laid far more than the Armani set!"

With increased popularity in New Age and the mass exodus away from traditional organized religions, the public seems to be very receptive to Krishna Dior's spiritual and fashion consciousness pitch.

Once again, for whatever reason, the Hare Krishna have not only attracted attention but have managed to secure an enthusiastic following. Is it the haircuts, their fashion line, the mystifying chants or a transcendental combination of all three? This is a question for the fashion historians to argue about. But if history teaches us one thing, it is this: If you dress funny, sing annoyingly loud, love thy neighbor as thyself and, most importantly, ask for the sale, you will attract enough followers and customers to make the cash register ring.

Krishna Dior's **Blue Mood Love Oil** ($69) available at Yaks Fifth Avenue or Dior to Door.

> **"**The amazing success of Krishna Dior is really something to chant about.**"**

Krishna Dior's **Tri-Eye sunglasses** because the third eye needs protection too! ($135)

Attention Valued Readers!

BUSINESS REPLY MAIL
FIRST-CLASS MAIL   PERMIT NO 666   BOULDER CO

POSTAGE WILL BE PAID BY ADDRESSEE

VAGUE

PO BOX 36-25-36
BOULDER COLORADO

NO POSTAGE
NECESSARY
IF MAILED
IN THE
UNITED STATES

We've nailed this annoying little subscription card onto the page so you won't bang your head on the coffee table while attempting to pick it up after it bounces off your crotch and happily flutters to the floor. Why are we being so nice to you? Well, it occurred to us that if you really wanted to frost our socks you could cause us a great deal of sorrow and financial strife. It costs us about 25 cents every time one of these subscription forms is returned to us—that really adds up. However, when people take a subscription to Vague we work the cost of processing into the price. But if everybody picked the business reply card up off the floor, marched it over to a mail box and dropped it in without filling out the handy address form on the back, we would end up getting charged for it. Now, we don't want to put any brainy ideas in your head, but here is the worst-case scenario. Every month one million annoying little cards are dropped into the mail box without a return address on them—we end up paying for

all of them without getting a lousy subscription out of it. Each month it costs us $250,000. Multiply that figure by twelve and over the course of a year we would lose $3 million. Our knees start to quiver and we're now shaking in our Gucchie booties. Now, multiply $3 million times three years and we have a full-scale epidemic on our hands. Perhaps even the end of fashion as we know it. So you can see why a few nails from the local hardware store are a small investment compared to what could happen if we didn't feel you were such a lovely group of body perfect women whom we love dearly. We can't begin to tell you what your responsible behavior and patronage mean to us. In fact, we wouldn't call you overweight and unattractive—even if you were. Besides, what does a little on the hefty side and not too pleasing to look at have to do with anything? So, if you follow the advice laid out in our editorial and buy all of the products advertised by our corporate sponsors, you could actually start enjoying a quality of life normally reserved for the "supermodels."

KRISHNA DIOR

FASHION CONSCIOUSNESS THAT'S SIMPLY DIVINE

when orange pants ruled the west

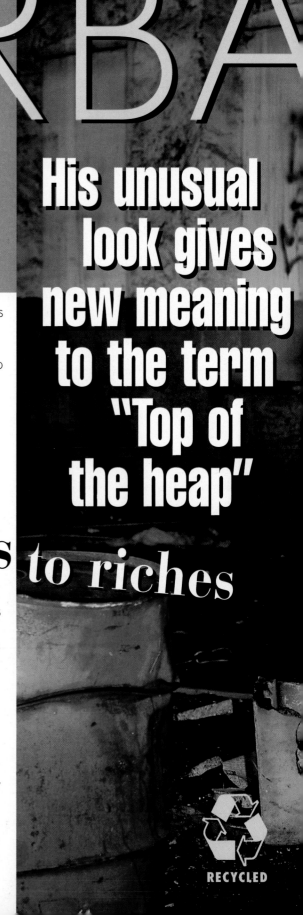

UMBERTO GARBA

THE DESIGNER WHO'S TURNING TRASH INTO CASH

When corporate downsizing came into business fashion it created a new niche in the fashion market place. This season Umberto Garbaggio's wardrobe downsize without compromise has helped ease the pain of the recession and is exciting news for the "Nouveau Impoverished."

With the celebrated release of his fabulous recycled materials collection, Umberto Garbaggio has reintroduced the "bag lady." His inspired designs are sure to stop traffic as well as cater to the budgets of the once affluent but recently fired. As waste disposal and recycling issues become more upfront and personal in our daily lives, his unusual look will give new meaning to the term "Top of the Heap."

from bags

"I insist on using only the finest rubbish. I wouldn't dream of scouring public dumps for cheaper waste materials and my clients can rest assured that items such as recycled colostomy bags are a definite no-no. They will never—even accidentally—find their way into my collections. I negotiate with reliable suppliers who pay special attention to each design detail—each specific requirement. I salvage and give old materials a rich, exciting, glamorous new look. Today's designers must be as resourceful as the customers they serve. Women who wear my collections are thrilled to discover they can still achieve the look of *rich-bitch* for thousands less."

His unusual look gives new meaning to the term "Top of the heap"

to riches

RECYCLED

GGIO

Vague photographer Stanislav Switalski surprises supermodels Nikki Tyler and Woo Paul on a dash-for-the-trash shopping spree at fashionable *Cul-de-Saks* on New York's Avenue E.

AGGIO

Nikki Tyler wearing used wedding car pom-poms woven into a tulle crinoline baby pouffe skirt ($595)

Top is clear and white plastic laminates filled with found trinkets ($425)

Pouffe You're Beautiful!

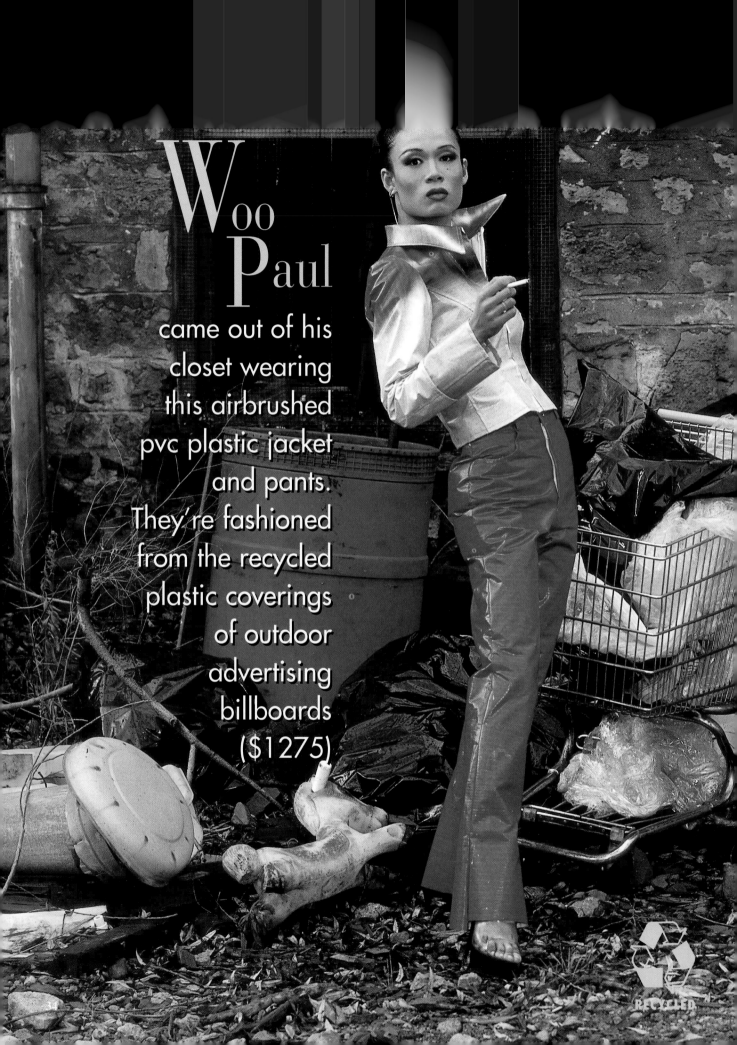

Woo Paul

Woo **P**aul came out of his closet wearing this airbrushed pvc plastic jacket and pants. They're fashioned from the recycled plastic coverings of outdoor advertising billboards ($1275)

RECYCLED

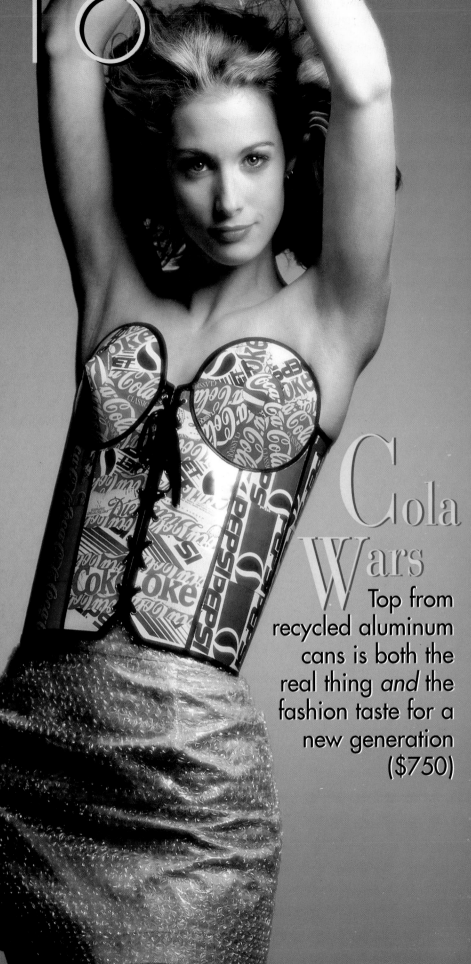

Cola Wars

Top from recycled aluminum cans is both the real thing *and* the fashion taste for a new generation ($750)

Pop My Bubbles

micro mini skirt is short on length and long on looks. Made from very rare, un-popped recycled bubble pack fabric ($395)

baby talk
for
The Tragically Hip

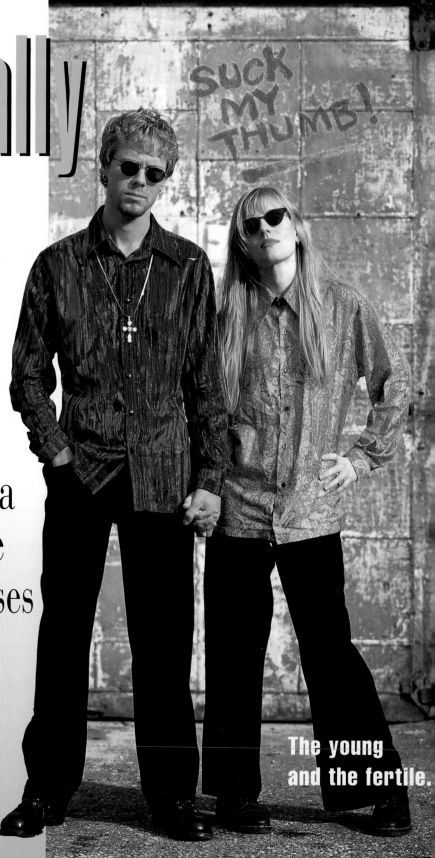

SUCK MY THUMB!

"There's a lot more **GOO** to a baby than the cute little noises they make."

The young and the fertile.

J ust when you thought you had it all—the loft in New York, the red Ferrari, extra cash and glamorous pretentious friends—along comes that one last nagging little fashion area—*babies!* For some, it might be an experience better left undiscovered.

Babies are fast becoming the fashion statement of the nineties. Easy to carry, great smelling head, available in a variety of chic shades. Still, as many people are finding out, there is a lot more goo to a baby than the cute little noises they make.

New York based psychiatrist Dr. Saul Lieberman, author of the critically acclaimed book *Here's The Poop On Babies!* has some interesting things to say about parenting in the late twentieth century.

The counseling clinic which Dr. Lieberman founded specializes in relationship dilemmas centered around child rearing. After years of counseling, he's amazed at the number of jaded couples having children just to be in fashion, or worse yet—popping one out in order to save a pathetic relationship.

Yet, many tragically hip couples are committing to poopy pants and pukey shoulders, convinced somewhere deep within them is a nurturing side waiting with arms outstretched. Says Lieberman, "People tell me they want a baby because they're cheap entertainment and, like, 'way cool!' When I hear this kind of talk, I am inwardly horrified. There are many hidden costs—for example, the cost of removing vomit from a velvet blouse or dry cleaning your silk slacks after a 'diaper overload' incident. Not to mention the damage to your hair where the baby chews on it. You have to look at the big picture."

Still worse, however, is the fact that the *kind* of attention garnered by a child can later be disappointing to the couple. Says Lieberman, "Many of the people who come to see me are frustrated about the impact that their new baby has had. Sure it draws interest, but it's all toward the baby. Ultimately, it is the baby who is fashionable, not the parents."

Is there a solution? Lieberman believes there is. He offers an unusual program in which he retrains men and women to look—and act—like babies. He believes it is critical for people to remember how dependent they themselves once were. The program is expensive, but it boasts astounding results. His approach may be

CONTINUED ON NEXT PAGE

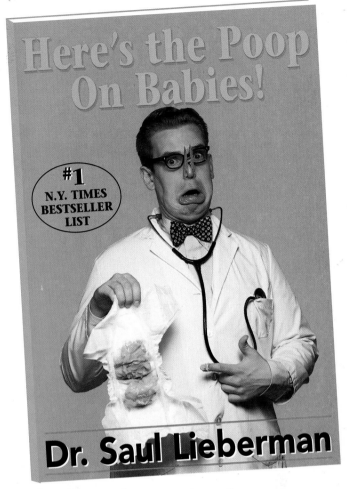

Here's the Poop On Babies!

#1 N.Y. TIMES BESTSELLER LIST

Dr. Saul Lieberman

" A relationship can last several years on good sex alone. But when the spark goes out, couples instinctively turn to parenthood. It's an ancient calling dating back to the monkeys which could end up driving them bananas. "

"We could find a fart in a hill of beans and we'd like to tell the world about it!"

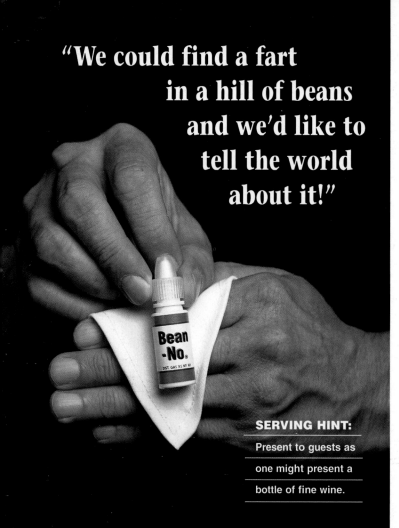

SERVING HINT:

Present to guests as one might present a bottle of fine wine.

It's true! One of life's most embarrassing little moments can now be controlled. Modern humans can say *pass* to gas before it erupts into a problem. We're of course referring to flatulence caused by beans, grains and gassy vegetables such as broccoli, peas and cauliflower. Just four or five drops on the first bite usually does the trick. Think of the freedom. When you just *have to* attend that hoity-toity soirée, Bean-No ® allows you to be there without having to frantically scan the room for an exit door, or worse yet, being left with no choice but to succumb to the moment and throw an accusing glance at a perfectly innocent stranger. With Bean-No, you can live with yourself, socialize with others, and nobody has to get hurt.

Bean-No ®

... If you know what we mean-o. ®

Available in fine stores and restaurants everywhere.

© Gas XS Inc.

CONTINUED FROM PREVIOUS PAGE

a little on the anal side for some, but when it comes to babies "shit happens" on a regular basis—get used to it.

The Dung and the Restless

Lieberman is the first to admit that graduating from his program will not be a cakewalk. "My methods require determination and stamina... You must poop your pants, go to work, walk around for an entire day. Stand, sit, sit, stand. Throw up on yourself. Poop 'em again! Pull a stranger's hair, stick your fingers up their nose, then pinch them making sure to direct your focus on only the tiniest, most sensitive areas of skin with untrimmed nails... Poop 'em some more... Throw up on a customer. Observe any unusual responses from your co-workers. Go home—but don't change your pants. Swallow an eraser, squash and eat a spider, be amazed by something shiny, then swallow it too. Yank on the dog's fur until he bites you—get stitches. Look for sympathy if there is any to be found. If you survive until bedtime, and you're still gripped by this urge to have a child, then there is either something seriously wrong with your sense of smell or you have other mental disorders. In either case you should make arrangements with my receptionist to have a thorough physical and a series of damn good psychotherapy sessions."

"Saying No! to Fruit Loops—just once—could cause an ugly scene and catapult you to number one on their shit list."

At $10,000 for the complete Lieberman program, it may be out of the financial range of many; but there are cheaper alternatives. The Egg in a Napkin Method is another exercise that's often used, where would-be parents must take care of an egg. They usually go through about twenty dozen of them and come away from the ordeal with yolk on their face doing the Cock-a-Doodle-doo-Me,* which lands them right back in the sack again with fertilization first and foremost on their minds.

Reasons for having a baby

1) "Oh my God!... Babies are, like, awesome! (2) Everyone else is having one. (3) We better have one now to get it over with. (4) Let's have two quick ones so that the first one will have someone to play with.

Reasons for not having a baby

(1) Babies make adults cranky. (2) You may make the mistake of teaching it everything *you* know. (3) You haven't lived yet. (4) Children are dependent and expensive, and the chances of them sticking a fork in an electrical outlet are fairly good. (5) It has all the trappings of modern day consumerism... you either buy tons of the right stuff or your child won't to be accepted by the other kids—and *you* won't be accepted by their parents... I believe the exact term is "fashionably at your wit's end."

---

* Cock-a-doodle-doo-me—like the Macarena only with your clothes off and without a condom.

If You Think She Whines Now
Just Wait Until She Grows Up
Gucchie
Goo ®
Damned expensive accessories
for spoiled little people.
© Gucchie Goo, a division of Gucchie International.
Gucchie Goo is a registered trademark of the Gucchie Corp.

Your pigskin jacket is now

Nothing is vulgar in nature.
Dans la nature rien n'est vulgaire.
自然のうちに、低俗なものは何もない。
Nada es vulgar en la naturaleza.
Ciò che è naturale non può essere volgare.
Nichts ist vulgär in der Natur.
自然就是美丽.

SCALPEL

When women flock from around the world to Rio de Janeiro to have their breasts enlarged, wrinkles erased and cellulite removed they come to see this man. He is Rio's Lipo King, Dr. Eduardo Rodriguez Exxon Valdez

He's the Rio Thing He's the Rio King

Reputation:
Most successful cosmetic surgeon in the world.

Achievements:
• Winner of Scalpelmania and current world champion belt holder.
• Founder and operator of *Retouch Tours Inc.*—a travel tour company which offers women all inclusive cosmetic surgery packages at his mountaintop clinic high above Rio.
• Inventor of LYPO KING— world's first home liposuction rental unit. LYPO KING is available in over 86 countries, at grocery and hardware chains. Find it beside the Do-it-yourself carpet-cleaning and Wet-Vac displays.

Clients:
Movie stars, young socialites, wives of imprisoned drug lords.

Specialties:
Liposculpture, face lifts, butt lifts, breast implants, tummy tucks and penis enlargements (size *does* make a difference).

Cost:
Who cares!!!!!!!!!!!!

Client Eligibility:
He does not conduct surgery on anyone who, in his sole opinion, is not physically, psychologically (or financially) stable. Women who want surgery to make their ex-husband's younger girlfriend jealous are politely told to come back next week when they've had some time to think—and when it's not quite so busy.

MANIA

What do you get when you take two hundred skilled cosmetic surgeons, four hundred patients, and thousands of screaming female fans, and you put them all in one huge stadium for a wacky, crazy, no-holds-barred slicefest? The answer, of course, is Scalpelmania—the sensational combination of microsurgery and wrestling that has taken Brazil by storm and now stands poised to conquer the rest of the world.

Many surgeons have made their names in this event, but the undisputed champion is Rio's Lipo King—Dr. Eduardo Rodriguez Exxon Valdez.

Four years ago, along with a group of his Brazilian contemporaries, Valdez founded the World Wide Federation of Cosmetic Surgeons (WWFCS). Their goal—to make plastic surgery more acceptable, more accessible, and above all more entertaining to the aging masses.

We caught up with the heartthrob Brazilian celebrity during one of his promotional tours, and asked him just what the event was all about.

Says Valdez, "Let me say at the outset that I am no sexist. Only after years of scientific study, did I discover that most women fantasize about walking down the beach in an up-the-ass thong bikini, basking in the attention that only a sexy body attracts. It's simple, they want large breasts and a sleek exterior – not raisins on a breadboard and a jigglefest! I also discovered a second thing. Women are inherently skeptical.

"Why put your breasts in anyone elses hands?"

Cosmetic surgery isn't cheap, and there is a perception that there are unknown risks involved. Before they undergo surgery themselves, they want to see somebody else try it first. It was to address these very legitimate concerns that we developed Scalpelmania." He rubs a silicone implant against his gyrating pelvis, then flings it into the outstretched arms of the crowd.

What started out as a gimmicky awareness-building campaign for plastic surgery has quickly exploded, catapulting appearance-altering surgery from a back alley clottage industry to the most popular medical sport on the planet.

For the third consecutive year, Scalpelmania has attracted over 160,000 women—and a growing number of men—to Rio de Janeiro's largest soccer coliseum. Here they witness the magic and mayhem of the world's finest surgeons as they slice through —and fight for—the coveted championship belt, as well as for the limited numbers of good-natured patients who pay top dollar to participate in the event.

Surgeons are judged on creativity, technical merit, endurance, and above all the ability to keep the audience entertained. Even if a patient dies on the operating table, the surgeon is not necessarily out of the running, provided that the manner of death was spellbinding or, at the very least, mildly amusing. It's a show with everything—sex, violence, and lots of money.

But Valdez wants people to realize that there's more to Scalpelmania than entertainment. "We also learn valuable medical techniques here," he says. "Take, for example, the fat that is extracted from liposuction. In the old days, it went to soap manu-

facturers, or was discarded as useless waste. But now, thanks to my research, we've found it be a most effective weapon. Whoosh! I throw it into the face of another surgeon, then Zzzwip! I snatch away his patient."

The American Medical Association has expressed its grave concerns about the Valdez approach. Says Dr. Paul Schnipit, a spokesman for the organization, "Scalpelmania is a travesty, a debasement of the medical arts. Here, in New York and Los Angeles combined, we have approximately 250 board-certified plastic surgeons. Over in Rio, they have more than 600! You can get anything done with state-of-the-art technology and for a fraction of the cost! Waaahhh! It's just not fair. It's time cosmetic surgery patients went back to shopping American, if for no other reason than value-added benefits. They get to sue our asses off for malpractice. Malpractice... now there's an American sport! I'd like to see the Brazilians follow that act. Unfortunately they can't; in Brazil, thanks to Scalpelmania, cosmetic surgery is now considered a contact sport. Malpractice suits are not allowed. Disfigurement, like any other sports injury, is deemed to be the risk you take for playing the game."

Valdez dismisses these concerns with a shrug. "Scalpelmania is a brilliant way for an industry to regulate itself. The best are rewarded with increased business; the hatchet job clinics are publicly humiliated or forced out of business. Our hometown crowds love us. Wealthy Brazilian women visit plastic surgeons more often than Americans visit the dentist," he says. "I'll tell you, a pleasant smile and a nice personality will barely get you 'hello' in Rio these days, but a thong bikini?—now that's what I call flossing!"

Valdez concedes that being a patient in Scalpelmania is not without its dangers. "Yes, you're going to get swelling. Yes, there is the risk of serious complications. Yes, you're going to lean towards "big hair" so that male suitors won't accidentally discover those tell-tale scars during the tender moments and heavy petting sessions. But if you can come away looking more beautiful—dead or alive—isn't it all worth it?"

The success of Scalpelmania shows clearly that the future belongs to plastic surgery. And age has little to do with it anymore. The ranks of patients have grown to include those in their early twenties who would like to regain the body of a teenager; those in their teens who would like to regain the body of a nine-year-old and even, according to Valdez, the occasional toddler who would like to, once again, achieve the supple body of a fetus.

Will Americans be able to catch up with Brazil's success? They will have a chance to find out this summer, when Valdez visits the Houston Astrodome to defend the belt in a challenge match against American penile, boob, buttock and facelift legend, Dr. Jimmy "The Masher" Mulligan, MD, MBSCSDD.

THINK OF IT AS BUYING A PAIR OF JEANS WITH A HAND ALREADY IN THEM

Things seem to happen when you wear Calvin Kline Jeans. Just owning a pair pretty much guarantees the wearer that "A Hot Time" is not too far away. Take a good look around and you'll see what we mean. After all, not all jeans were created equal. Next time you see a pair of jeans that are, like, too hot to trot yet too cool to not; chances are Calvin Kline has had a hand in them.

Calvin Kline
Jeans
The hand goes in before the name goes on.®

Vague living Doggy

Why a Jack Russell Terrier is better than a man

f your spouse spends most of his time in the doghouse anyway, why not just get a dog?

All the sticks he can fetch, candlelight squirrel dinners, and nobody steps foot on the porch without a damn good reason. For the woman who wants a partner who will not only provide dinner but is also willing to go out and kill it, a Jack Russell Terrier could be her ticket.

'Sit pretty,' 'roll over and play dead,' 'shake a paw' and 'stay,' could all soon be within every woman's grasp. It's as simple as making one convenient phone call to the Jack Russell Terrier Club.

Perhaps you're skeptical about four-legged companionship? Don't be. It's more familiar than you think. Every woman at one time or another has been in the company of a man who has come crawling in on all fours at 2 a.m. Whether the occasion was drunkenness or shameless begging for another chance (or both), we've all been there once. Can you recall those times? Remember how tall you felt? Wow! He barely came up to your knees. Soon you could experience this luxury every day of the year. Believe it! Four little paws going click, click, click across the kitchen floor could be a sound you will grow to trust and love.

If you're asking yourself, 'What am I getting into?' then this is a very positive sign. It means you're finally growing up. And to be sure that you grow in the right direction Vague has compiled the following comparative look at men and their four-legged rivals. It may help you decide if *Jack* is a name you could come home to.

Unlike a man, a Jack Russell is easy to train. He's intelligent and wiry. A little kibble goes a long way in the loyalty department. You never have to worry about him leaving the toilet seat up after he goes. Or worse yet—leaving it down before he goes. He may drink out of the toilet several times a week, but then your ex probably did too. And while you may not be turned on by the parts of himself that he licks, at least he won't ask you to do it.

A Jack Russell will bark at the neighbor's cat—your husband did as well but you weren't aware of it. Both are instinctively territorial, marking their turf by peeing on fire hydrants and property lines; men just don't do it in front of you. Both will howl at night, but the beauty of a Jack Russell is you can yell 'shut up!' and you won't have it thrown back in your face three weeks later. Although it's common practice to train both dogs *and* men to 'stay,' training a man to 'stay'

is one thing; training him to 'stay home' is quite another.

If a Jack Russell ever comes on too strong with the jumping on the leg thing, simply drop him off at the vet for the *big snip,* and within twenty-four hours you'll be amazed at how subservient he becomes. You can now relax, lie back on the couch, stuff your face with bonbons while he licks the calluses off your feet—the novelty never wears off.

If you ever want to get rid of a dog all you have to do is feed him chicken bones and go away for the weekend... If it was only that simple to get rid of a man.

If your spouse is the type who disapproves of the way you dress it's comforting to know that a Jack Russell doesn't care how short you wear your skirt. They can see up all of them anyway.

Jack Russells can smell a rat a mile away. (Yes! Yes! Couldn't we all have used one years sooner.) And here's a bonus: when you're really tired, a dried smoked pig's ear (male chauvinist or otherwise) will entertain them for hours.

> "training a man to 'stay' is one thing; training him to 'stay home' is quite another."

No Monday night baseball, football, basketball, cricket. You wanna be a bitch to him? Not a problem. They were raised by bitches. The bigger the better. If you happen to call him a son-of-a-bitch it's practically a term of endearment; the equivalent of saying, "Well, aren't you mommy's little boopy today!"

And now the clincher: no in-laws! The only thing that comes with a Jack Russell is a pedigree. An attractive, harmless piece of paper which simply states that he *has* parents. Parents who will never ever visit, or worse yet pressure you about producing grandchildren.

Well, ladies, if you haven't already yanked the phone off the wall trying to phone about pups, what the hell are you waiting for? No sports, no in-laws, the clicker stays under your control, and a little puppy follows you home everyday. Are you daft? Pick up the phone and call now! That toll-free number is 1-800-HERE-BOY.

Style

Could the perfect man for the job be man's best friend?

The slice of life

Most women believe deep down inside that circumcision doesn't go far enough.

When it comes to their wieners, men are a little on the protective side lately. It shouldn't come as a surprise, considering that only a short while ago the media made celebrities out of Loreena and John Wayne Lobbitt.

To refresh your memory: she took a knife and lobbed off his penis. He found it, had it sewn back on. The media and the legal system took over and the public got the blow by blow from the comfort and safety of their living rooms. Men watched in horror, women reacted with thunderous applause. The couple's fifteen minutes of fame was a financial success and has prompted males worldwide to sleep with one eye open, on their tummies, in their pajamas—with the fly securely buttoned.

The Lobbitt *can of worms* raises some important questions. Should couples who invest their emotional life savings in a dysfunctional relationship be allowed to cash in on their investment? Should the public be forced to watch them wash and air their dirty laundry and precious unmentionables over the public airwaves? And last but not least, *do* inquiring minds *really* want to know? According to the tabloids, TV magazine shows and opinion polls, "Yes they do!"

Apparently we want to know what she was thinking. Whether she was drinking. How she handled the evidence. Did she toss it out of a speeding automobile at the outskirts of town? Was it a world famous Ginsu Ever Sharp knife which dealt the final slice? And if it was, will it still slice a tomato without mushing it, and give you perfect julienne vegetables—every time? Is this the *real* reason it isn't available in stores?

Right or wrong, the landmark case was a wakeup call for men. It was over so fast they never got a chance to hit the snooze button. The goldfish had eaten the cat. A most disturbing turn of events, but the message comes through loud and clear. Most women believe, deep down inside, that circumcision doesn't go far enough. This spells D-I-S-A-S-T-E-R for men who think with their penises instead of their brains.

Barbie And Ken

Penis removal isn't a big leap for women, considering that most little girls grow up playing with Barbie dolls and believe that boys are supposed to be smooth down there like Barbie's friend Ken.

Instead of feeling sorry for Ken they throw a pair of pants on him, a loud shirt, and off they go to meet Barbie, who's upset because she's got panty line and angry that *Ken* is two hours late.

Some toy industry psychologists are proposing that, in future, all dolls be anatomically correct so it's more of a hurdle for women. They want to ensure that this constant exposure to men without penises doesn't put crazy ideas into their heads and, in an effort to maintain public health and safety, are putting pressure on toy companies to make a few minor additions.

Let's forget for a moment, as Loreena Lobbitt did, that unconsenting penis removal is not only an act of violence, but also against the law and damned unsportsmanlike. If a woman cuts off her man's penis, what does she personally stand to lose?

Sex is definitely out of the question. This may well be a blessing, depending on the individual. Pretty dresses and bouquets of flowers—gone! Romantic candlelit dinners for two? What's the point?

It appears that most of the niceties in a relationship go out the window. By now it's far too late. Everything has healed up and smoothed over. So, how does one begin again? You might attempt gluing it back on, but if it doesn't fix a broken handle on a teacup it probably won't mend a severed penis—not to mention the fact that it will never be dishwasher safe again.

A Stitch In Time Saved Mine...

GOOD NEWS FOR MEN – With all the attention being given to unauthorized surgery there is good news for war-torn couples who have allowed the moment to get away on them but who are also willing to immediately address the matter. It's The Penis Reattachment Kit™ for home, office or auto.

It's been hailed as a glorious second chance and a minor surgical miracle wonder. It offers distraught amputees and their angry (but beginning to stabilize) girlfriends the flexibility to piece and stitch their tattered lives back together without involving the police and further antagonizing the neighbors.

The kit comes with easy to follow instructions and is so simple you'll wonder why doctors are paid so much for something that a complete moron can do. The amputee himself will be able to negotiate the twists, loops, turns and stitches like a seasoned professional, and it's a sure-fire way to get men to learn how to sew.

There is never a good excuse for marital violence. There is always the door. Male or female, big or petite, we all have the power to choose. The Penis Reattachment Kit is effective, but it's only a band-aid on something which could once again raise its ugly head and strike back without warning.

For the woman who is tired of the *bull* and longs to have her life back, she may want to consider taking the bull by the horns and kicking his ass out the door. It's an interesting alternative to castration and a lot less painful in the long run for both parties, particularly for the bull.

If all else fails, do as Loreena did. Go for the groin, go for the talk show circuit, and, yes, go for the cash! It works every time. Remember, after all, inquiring minds *do* want to know.

A Diamond Lasts Forever...
A failed marriage lasts an eternity and usually ends in divorce.

"The Rock"
At fine jewelers everywhere.

"It ain't over *even* when it's over."

Ahh! The *wooly pants* of divorce. There's no fit like 'em and they always seem to have your size in stock. No waist too large or small, no inseam fit too short or tall.

These are the same itchy, wooly pants everyone silently reserves for themselves when they go shopping for a diamond ring with a recommended budget of two months' salary.

To reserve your pair, call the Jewelers of America and ask for their free brochure on *How To Buy a Diamond.* Go ahead and take the plunge. But remember this, when the pool is cold and you can't tread water for longer than a *big wet kiss*, a little financial safety net is *always* in fashion.

One Anvil
gets rid of even the worst headaches.

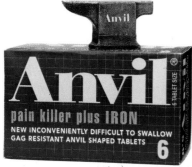

VAGUE OFFER

Welcome to
YOU LOOK MARVELOUS
Population 1

How to apply makeup while driving

A rearview approach for applying makeup in your car.

At last, something for women to do in the *front* seat of a car that won't mess up her hair, wrinkle her skirt or ruin her reputation.

More and more women realize that you don't get a second chance to make a first impression. With time being precious and circumstances being unpredictable, an auto makeover is often the most intelligent choice you can make.

Looking good doesn't happen by accident, and if it does, it can only mean that you never did your homework... *VAGUE* will get you to that next engagement, on time, in one piece and looking like a million bucks.

VAGUE beauty experts, posing as crash test dummies, racked up more than two hundred career auto accidents to perfect this fabulous new program—and have more stitches than a baseball glove to show for it.

It's no longer just a theory that women labor harder, longer and more efficiently than their male counterparts. As a result, they find themselves in a state of perpetual hurriedness. But unless they are prepared to adopt time management skills in the area of primping, preening and pampering, they will be unable to make it into work, on-schedule, looking businesslike *and* feminine.

The **VAGUE** External Beauty Video Series

Tape #1
How To Apply Makeup While Driving

"One video improves concentration and shows how to maximize valuable time that used to be wasted on minding the road and watching out for crazy drivers"

"Take it off and get it on while driving to work and still keep your virginity."

You'll learn how to apply a professional makeup job while observing the rules of the road. All things considered, a makeover done in the car is as safe as conventional methods *and* less expensive. It also frees up more time to finish the backlog of work at your job or allows you that simple luxury of an extra hour of beauty sleep.

Vague Makeover Tips

You'll Discover:
* How to use *cruise control* before you *lose control*.
* How to handle Blush Hour Traffic.
* The difference between a compact and a sub-compact.
* Eyebrow maintenance—avoiding trucks between the plucks.
* How to steer the car by the thigh, knee and elbow method.

Video only $79.99

Now turn your car into a salon-on-wheels. Make each second count. Speed up the transformation process by choosing from a quality line of professional auto makeover accessories. Each item is installed by a trained professional and is guaranteed for as long as you own your car.

Options include:
* Driver's side footbath and aqua pulsator.
* Hot & Cold running water.
* Driver's side hairbag and waste disposal unit.
* Salon-style hair drier replaces head rest on driver's seat.
* Dashboard-mounted nail grinder, buffer, polisher, drier.
* Driver's seat hip and thigh jiggler massage unit.
* Dash-mounted professional cosmetic tool kit with the latest innovations in makeup.
* Giant rearview vanity mirror with over fifty lights—allows you to observe facial construction *and* motorists behind you who may be riding your butt.
* Trucker-style emergency-warning air horn makes blowing through an intersection on a red light a breeze.
* And much, much more.

Buy the video and ask for your free accessory catalogue today!
Call now to order: 1-800-ERR-RRT!
VAGUE has a network of installation & service centers nationwide.

why STOP
do it while you drive

& Sexy Slippery

Good Looking Guys with Great Tans

Leaning on Shovels Next 20 Miles

SLOW
Make Over Zone Ahead

Facial Reconstruction
Next 5 Miles

BUMPS
apply eyeliner with caution

Men Playing with Balls
Caution

YIELD
to younger men

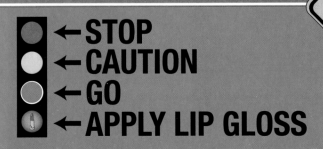
← STOP
← CAUTION
← GO
← APPLY LIP GLOSS

Veggie t Dips

"Somewhere between Ponce de León and a facelift lies a low-tech method of achieving a younger-looking complexion."

They're not just for snacking anymore. In fact, many women are finding that by dipping into the dips there is less chance of dipping into their life savings to bankroll the more expensive surgery. But are these natural remedies really all they're cracked up to be?

Juan Ponce de León was the 16th century explorer who boldly went where countless others had gone before, hoping to find the one thing everyone else had overlooked—the legendary Fountain of Youth.

History has not been kind to Ponce de León—even his contemporaries thought he was crazy. Maybe it was his obsession with this place he called *Floreeda*, or finding a permanent cure for the aging process. Perhaps this was why people snickered when he passed them on the street.

Fortunately for Poncey, madness was also rampant among the nobility and royalty of the day, and they gladly financed his dream expedition to the tune of fifty thousand gold doubloons, eight chests of jewelry, and last and by every means least: a freight container of worthless trinkets which would be given to the godless natives in exchange for *their* gold and *their* women.

With laser surgery more than 500 years away, Ponce de León and his preposterous vision was his investor's only hope. The promise was alluring. His clients had but to immerse themselves in the fragrant waters of the Fountain of Youth, and all trace of age would vanish from their bodies. (None of that, "Hey! This spring smells like farts!" therapeutic sulfer water stuff for this elite, pampered group.)

The treatment was to be offered at no charge—except for the passage to Florida on one of the Fleet de León galleons, and three weeks' accommodation in the beautiful, luxurious five-star Palace de Ponce Hotel (now owned and operated under the Hilton banner).

Ponce de León guaranteed the consortium of venture capitalists that his discovery would deliver eternal youthfulness *and* a perpetual erection. (This last point clinched the financing!)

Today, Florida is known as the retirement capital of North America and is living proof that Ponce de León was off-his-flipping-rocker. Although his cause was fueled by the usual greed, you can't blame a man for trying.

It comes as no surprise, then, that Ponce de León died as many of us will: of old age... and of syphilis, I might add. Not even bathing in the Fountain of Youth would have saved him.

(How you come clean has little influence on longevity, but if you insist on getting dirty with the wrong people it'll bury you every time.)

Now, as we stand on the doorstep of the third millennium, beauty experts still search for the fountain of youth. So far they have only managed to produce reasonable facsimiles. Many cosmetic manufacturers believe that somewhere between Ponce de León and a facelift lies a low-tech, cost-effective method of achieving a younger-looking complexion.

First there was Retin-A, originally designed to fight acne but now used to eliminate wrinkles and lines. This was followed by Retina, which does nothing to the wrinkles themselves, but blurs your vision so that you can no longer see them. Then came Alpha hydroxy acids, an acid peel compound which had failed miserably in the autobody industry but found new success removing "old paint" of another kind.

Now the latest skin care craze is vitamins! vitamins! vitamins! Vitamins C, E and beta-carotene act as antioxidants and help the body break up and dispose of "free radicals." (Possibly what the National Guard used against the hippies in the 1960s.)

These vitamin products are designed for the busy woman who doesn't have the financial resources for surgery or the time to slice fruit and vegetables, place them on her face and wait for results. By applying high concentrations of vitamins C and E in cream form, women will no longer have to worry about finishing their veggies in order to achieve their just desserts... blah blah blah... A REALISTIC-SOUNDING CLAIM... blah blah blah... IF IT COSTS MORE IT WORKS BETTER... blah blah blah... AGING IS A SERIOUS DISEASE... blah blah blah... ACCIDENTALLY MISTAKEN FOR AN EIGHTEEN YEAR OLD... blah blah blah... IT'S AN AMAZING COMPOUND... blah blah blah... IS THAT YOUR SISTER OR YOUR DAUGHTER?... blah blah blah... THANKS! HERE'S TWENTY BUCKS... blah blah flippin' blah.

Although in recent years there have been great advancements in the field of medicine, it may be too little too late for the present generation. Modern-day research is fueled by huge advertising budgets and the usual greed. However, unless we can come up with some concrete solutions, or locate and alter the gene responsible for aging, we risk sharing the same fate as Ponce de León (preferably without the syphilis), or worse yet, dying from an overdose of carrots.

Great
for
picky
eaters!

Vague interview

With Karl Lagerhead
by contributing writer Iszada Minkstol

Karl Lagerhead has many, many fans. Some must be plugged in, some are battery operated, some require gentle wrist action, some even have adjustable speed control *and* a heater setting.

In this issue we visit *Grand Chump*, Lagerhead's magnificent mansion in Brittany where Vague contributing writer Iszada Minkstol talks to the crown prince of contemporary design in the midst of his spectacular fan collection. He shares his most intimate thoughts and insights about the role of fashion and the role of today's designers, and even offers us some philosophical wisdom.

Vague: You have been described by your critics as a riddle, wrapped in a mystery, inside an enigma, on top of fashion with a dollop of je ne sais quoi on the side. Is this a fair assessment?

Lagerhead: I am not understanding your words... but as long as people are talking about *me* it is pleasing to my ears. I will take "enigmatic" over "smart ass ninny with the ponytail" any day of the week.

Vague: Many of these same critics say that some of your inspirations have been plagiarized from the world of rock music. Is there any truth to these accusations?

Lagerhead: Will these slanders never end? My "Nirvana" grunge collection came out weeks before the group became popular. You have to ask yourself, *why* did Kurt Cobain kill himself? Was it really a combination of drugs and an overpowering sense of futility, or was it the shame of having stolen my "look." This has happened to me before. My "Sid Vicious" collection, my "Jimi Hendrix" collection—all of these stolen by rock stars who just happened to have the same names... Oh yes, I will take smart ass ninny with the ponytail over plagiarizer any day of the week!

Vague: So you haven't been influenced in any way by the rock world?

Lagerhead: If you are implying that I'm inspired by someone wiggling their derriere at a concert then you are partly right... but it is the wiggle itself that is the inspiration, not *what* the wiggle is wearing.

❝If fashion messes its pants it is zee responsibility of zee designers to change it. Whoever created zee baby must change zee diapers.❞

Vague: So a gyrating pelvis triggers something in your head. Phallic pencil meets vulnerable wide-open sketch pad, and a new collection is conceived?

Lagerhead: Yes! Yes! That is it exactly. I like that. I may use that. In fact, I thought of *that* myself—weeks ago.

Vague: What about the clothes themselves?

Lagerhead: Let me say only this. Ultimately, fashion is not about being covered up. It is about becoming naked. The clothes, then, are a means to an end—a bare end.

Vague: Are you saying that people get dressed so they can get undressed?

Lagerhead: This is precisely so.

Vague: That they *buy* robes in order to be *dis*robed.

Lagerhead: Yes, this is the inescapable naked truth about life.

Vague: Has it *always* been this way?

Lagerhead: Always. The genesis of fashion began with Adam and Eve; today's designers owe their careers to sin. This is why we don't feel bad when we create a naughty collection. Adam and Eve were the first models to walk down the runway, although it was probably more like sneaking and running. But if you insist on eating from the tree of life and knowledge zen baby you better be prepared to run for cover.

Vague: So fashion has helped take some of the shame out of being naked?

Lagerhead: We have no shame. When free sex got popular, fashion became its publicity director, and as much as the world loves to look fabulous we just can't wait to tear it all off and exercise our shameful primal instincts.

Vague: So, then, fashion is a language of sorts?

Lagerhead: Precisely! We are all bilingual as soon as we become fashion conscious—even before. People dress to get what they want. Children annoy parents, women wear slinky skirts to make their boyfriends jealous. Each style, every look, makes a statement. They are tools we use to improve our position: in business, in pleasure, in love.

We must be careful what our fashion says to others. Zat wiggly derriere might just sell you down the river without any means of return... I sink the English expression is, up zis place you call "Shit's Creek" without any fans. The wrong fashion statement in the wrong company... oh yes, a woman can quite easily become a magnet for creeps.

Vague: What's this new minimalism of yours all about?

Lagerhead: Simplicity. You will see my *Fresh from the Shower Collection* in this

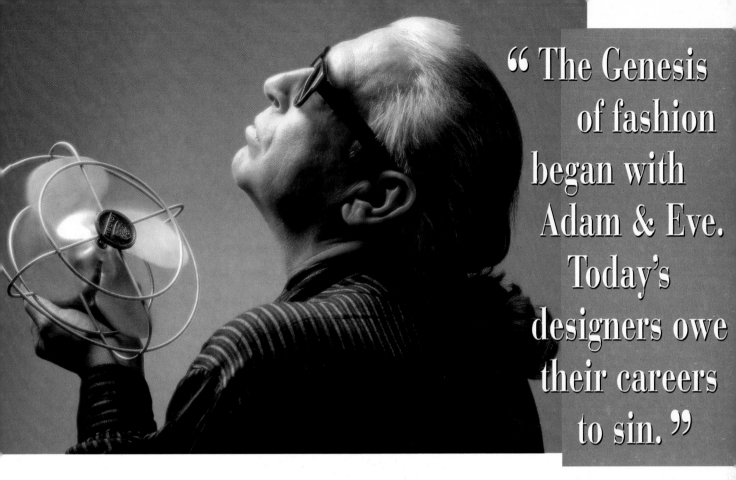

> " The Genesis of fashion began with Adam & Eve. Today's designers owe their careers to sin. "

issue. What could be more simple than emerging from the shower and, while still dripping wet, wrap yourself in a towel, and off you go to the airport, onto a waiting flight—destination unknown. It is bold, radical, free, unconventional styling. It is the *least* you can do.

Vague: Because of cost, your clothes are not for everyone. Which niche markets do you go after?

Lagerhead: Obviously, because my collections are genius they appeal to a higher caliber of clientele... the annoyingly spoiled, the significantly heeled and the stinking rich... How's that for niche marketing?

Vague: Impressive... so what happens when fashion fails to live up to the expectations of the public?

Lagerhead: If fashion messes its pants it is zee responsibility of zee designers to change it. Whoever created zee baby must change zee diapers—it's that simple.

Vague: I heard that you have vivid dreams. Do you ever design from them?

Lagerhead: Yes, I even design *in* my sleep. I had a dream about the creative process only last night. I was in the emergency waiting room at the hospital. I was not alone. Scattered around me were my designer peers: Jean-Paul Goatcheese, Umberto Garbaggio, Jean Claude Clod, to name a few. We were all dreadfully ill. The head administrator refused us medical attention until someone could come up

with a better, more flattering original design for hospital uniforms. And so the contest began. We were informed that one designer would be chosen, the rest would perish in the midst of the common people, die in a sea of sore throats, black eyes, broken arms and twisted ankles. We all began sketching madly in order that we might be first, to be fashion's chosen one...

Vague: It sounds frightening.

Lagerhead: It *was* frightening. I began drawing big funny nun hats with immense wings, women in unusual outfits—I gave them all huge asses... I kept rushing up to the admittance counter like a child races home with a report card. I was scolded for drawing big asses, but I only draw what I see. It was as if this special part of the anatomy was speaking to me—a revelation. Suddenly it became clear; it isn't how big the ass is but how you present it. Some women have big asses but don't view them as a curse. The ass plays an important role. It speaks long before your mouth opens. As you walk along it says "Bonjour, hello, I'm free for dinner if you are brave enough to ask." It upsets me that women let their asses get the best of them. One thing that separates youth from middle age is attitude. If the mind goes downhill the body follows like an avalanche. The mind must stay positive. Women shouldn't take themselves out of the running so soon...

Vague: And where was that war-witch of

an administrator through all of these ponderings?

Lagerhead: Probably reflecting on her ass... So anyway, I scurried back to the administrator and said you are going to love what I've done for your ass. She was taken aback at first, but remarkably she did love it and it was her ass I was drawing all along. A great design makes all the difference— find the right look and you have success... And then I awoke in my bed at home.

Vague: These designs you create in your sleep—do you go on to sell them?

Lagerhead: Oh, yes. I sold 40,000 of those nun's hats.

Vague: In Europe?

Lagerhead: No—this was in the dream.

Vague: What else have you learned from your dreams?

Lagerhead: Look your best and don't give up. I don't necessarily subscribe to the idea that anatomy is destiny, although *Baywatch* never lost popularity because of firm bodies... Ultimately you must be glad with what you have and work with what you've got.

Vague: Karl Lagerhead the philosopher? I'm impressed.

Lagerhead: And I'm impressed by your perceptiveness—and that's impressive because I'm never impressed.

Vague: You are marvelous

Lagerhead: No, *you* are... OK, you're right, I *am*.

Lettuce Alone

gets the desired reaction.
Jean Claude Clod creates the look
that grows on you, turning heads and
leaving them green with envy.
Mother always said if
you didn't eat your
vegetables you'd
end up wearing
them. ($1295)

Hat Couture

The genius of Jean Claude Clod

"If your hat is stunning enough you should be able to walk around naked without anyone noticing... Later, what lies below your brow can rather conveniently become the topic of conversation but only, of course, after they stop complimenting you on zee hat." —Jean Claude Clod

Just when you thought it was safe to go out without a hat, Jean Claude Clod redefines "Hat Couture." His stunning designs are inspiring women to reach even greater heights. Today it's not so much what's *inside* your head but what's on top of it that counts. These fabulous châpeaus are not only prompting women to wear hats, but many of them are wearing little else and getting away with it.

Dressed to Grill

Watch the heads rotate this party-going season as you walk in wearing Jean Claude Clod's hottest new creation. The comments will be endless as you rekindle an old flame, or smolder away in the arms of someone new... Where there's smoke there's fire. ($1900)

All Fired Up

"I've taken care of the entrée... the dessert will be up to you!?!"

–Jean Claude Clod

EYE-FULL TOWER
Hat

The height of style
—the style of height

Jean Claude Clod's
Eiffel Tower creation,
hand-crafted from
authentic medical tongue
depressors and popsicle
sticks, gives the admirer
more than one reason
to "say ahhhh!"
Now, tower above
the crowd in this
limited edition
châpeau.
($3000)

C'est Ahhhhh!

Vague arts

Tantrum Art Is Smashing Success

A member of a dysfunctional family herself, Scandinavian-born artist Ona Rampage is gaining quite a reputation at home and abroad with her touring gallery exhibition "Picking Up The Pieces."

early in her marriage Ms. Rampage became a hurler and a smasher. To make matters worse, she is ambidextrous. Like a human twister, her fits of rage would consume an entire room in a palpitating heartbeat.

Trapped in a hopeless, loveless relationship, the walls became her palette, frustration her inspiration, and Svën... Svën was her dörk of a husband who helped make her nightmare and dreams come true. Without Svën there would have been no anger, no art, no story.

What sets her apart from the ordinary, everyday, pedestrian psychotic is how she dealt with the aftermath. While sweeping up following each session, she found it difficult to discard the pieces; she felt drawn to arrange it into artistic order.

"Anger management classes may be great for some—but I'm far more creative when I'm pissed off."

Her autobiographical best seller *Svën is a Dörk: Picking Up the Pieces*. Ona Rampage, Rangdom House Publishers. Available at book stores everywhere.

Ona Rampage rolled up her sleeves and waded into the nightmare one piece at a time. Working with shards of glass, metal fragments, and other debris from the living hell she once knew, she created an impressive road map back from the depths of despair. For the first time in her life she experienced a calm; like the relief which follows the lancing of a boil, the anger had vanished, the pressure gone.

Rampage is truly one of a kind: married at 21, frustrated by 22, psychotic at 23 (beginning of the productive years), separated at 27, rich and famous at 28, divorced at 29. Women worldwide can learn something from her example.

Then there was Svën. Jealous of her recognition, he sued for his portion of her income, claiming that he was the catalyst for the anger, the inspiration behind her success. The court awarded Svën a settlement of $1.2 million.

Rampage's reaction to the upset decision? She shrugs. "It's an upset, but I'm used to being upset. I guess I feel surprise, disappointment and kind of a burning anger which is like a living entity within me, you know." We do indeed, Ona! Sounds like more inspiration for those cool 'n' crazy creations!

Svën Is A Dörk
PICKING UP THE PIECES
Ona Rampage

horoscopes

By Agatha Starchild M.V.E.M.J.S.U.N.P.

t

he planets and their position in the solar system profoundly affect the events and fortunes we experience in our everyday lives. It's cosmically bewildering, at times causing even me to ask, "What does it all mean?" Take the letters following my name, for instance. Not only do they represent several prestigious and hard-earned astrological degrees from the American Matchbook Learning Academy, they also, quite by chance, happen to stand for the names of the planets in the solar system.

A strange coincidence, you may think. But it doesn't end there. The names of the planets can also be remembered using the little acronym "Mary Very Early Made Jerry Stand Up Nearly Perpendicular." I learned it back in elementary school and thought little of it—until my friend Mary met a guy named Jerry and did indeed make him stand up nearly perpendicular. Truly, the heavens influence everything we do.

Vague has a surprise for those ladies who never listened in elementary school and made it through life thus far on personality alone. We are going to divulge the names of the planets to this elite group. Here they are in order of appearance and proximity to the Sun. Ladies and otherwise... the amazing and powerfully influential planets of the solar system as we know it: Mercury, Venus, Earth, Mars, Jupiter, Saturn, Uranus, Neptune and Pluto.

I would like to clarify, on behalf of our very timid readers, that the word chosen for the planet Uranus has nothing to do with what you may think it sounds like it might have something to do with—if you catch my intergalactic drift. Although the wonders of the human anatomy are at times way out there, you'll be relieved to know that Uranus is just Uranus and has nothing to do with Uranus.

Disclaimer: The advice and predictions appearing in this section are the opinions and beliefs of the writer and do not necessarily reflect the opinions and beliefs of Vague Magazine, despite the fact that we *do* sign her paychecks.

Aquarius *(January 20–February 18)*

Your entire life has been one big extended "Oh my God! I forgot to take the casserole out of the oven!" However, this is the least of your worries as once again Aquarians are going to end up carrying a lot of water this month. Yes, that's what the jug is for! Aquarians are not strangers to water retention; it's the one thing you're really good at. The word bloat doesn't even have to come up. We're 98% water anyway, so don't be concerned. This flashy fleshy container we carry around with us is just God's way of reminding us that he does indeed have a unique sense of humor.

Pisces *(February 19–March 20)*

The good news is—you're creative. The bad news is—you're about as flaky as grilled Atlantic salmon. You went overboard a long time ago Pisces and have been quite successfully treading water ever since. Don't ask for special consideration; it wouldn't be fair to the other signs. I'm running a horoscope column here, not a Department of Social Services. There will be no handouts *this* month or any other month. What Pisces does with this anchor around her neck is entirely up to Pisces. You jumped into a kettle of fish all on your own. Now let's just see if you're creative enough to get yourself out. If you want to swim with the big fish you can't spend your life floating about with the guppies.

Aries *(March 21–April 19)*

Enzo down at the butcher shop is probably going to propose again this month. There is something attractive about Italians that goes beyond linguine in a clam sauce, but I haven't quite figured it out yet. And as much as Enzo is a pest, there is something magnetic about a man in a blood-drenched apron surrounded by beef tongue, wieners, t-bones and strip loins. It won't hurt to invite him over for dinner, but be careful. An apron like that could accidental-

ly lead you to a career in television and a series of stain-removing laundry detergent commercials. Although the residuals may pay handsomely, is "Leave It to Cleaver" the guy you really want? And will the fruits of his loins ever be enough to sustain a satisfying and comfortable lifestyle for you?

Taurus *(April 20–May 20)*

Don't be walked over by people who are wealthier and more influential than you. Taurus doesn't have to tolerate the bull anymore. It's time to take charge. You will be amazed and delighted at what you can actually receive from others these days by merely sticking a loaded revolver in their rib cage. If you can master the ten little magic words: "Down on the floor and nobody has to get hurt!" you are well on your way to financial independence. It's a *bull market,* Taurus; time to trade places.

Gemini *(May 21–June 21)*

How appropriate! You look in the mirror and suddenly realize that you either *have* a twin or you're about to give birth to twins. Liposuction is probably the only cure this side of liking yourself as you are. Liposuction is a memorable experience. You won't need an anesthesic; the sound alone is enough to knock you out. After its discovery, the inventing surgeons, realizing they couldn't just call it a fat-sucking vacuum cleaner for humans, asked themselves, "Well what shall we name this exciting new process?" They arrived at the name by allowing themselves to be inspired by the actual noise generated by the process itself. LLLLL-yyy-p-p-po-po-po-s-s-s-u-u-u-c-c-c-c-shun. After several hours of facial aerobics and rude sucking noises, the word liposuction just sort of jumped out at them. It's truly amazing what you can invent when all you have at your disposal is a vacuum pump, some tubing and a nozzle. Of course a lineup out the door and down the hallway is very inspirational as well. Proving that *greed*, not *necessity*, is the true mother of invention.

TAURUS:

If you can master the ten little magic words: "Down on the floor and nobody has to get hurt!" you are well on your way to financial independence.

Cancer *(June 22 - July 22)*

Crabs are itchin' to be bitchin' this month. Well, drama lovers, isn't it about time you started to agitate someone? On the 9th of this month you will once again catch your partner blowing his nose in the shower and attempting to get the snot off his fingers by a process known as rinse and flick. If men were more like a good shampoo—rich, gentle and non-irritating—we'd all be a lot better off. Even if they were to take the first step in a new direction and be more like a premium beer—rich, full-bodied, aged to perfection and mature in only six weeks—it would be encouraging and an indication to women that they will not be spending the rest of their lives babysitting a child who makes sexual advances.

Leo *(July 23–August 22)*

It's a jungle out there and the lioness is hungry this month. Time to forget the diet. Go out and splurge. Kill yourself a zebra. Cut a straggler from the herd. One of the weak ones. What the hell, the Serengeti belongs to you. Around the 7th, be more like the giraffe. If you want the tender leaves on those really high branches you're going to have to stick your neck out. Don't wait for evolution to bail you out. Reach up and grab it, Leo! Come on! You're dealing with greenery here! It's easier than you think. On the 15th, hyenas will try to steal your kill but this time *you* get the last laugh. Indeed, the lioness *must* stay on her toes this month.

Virgo *(August 23–September 22)*

Cosmetic surgery is on the horizon. Leave it there! If your curiosity gets the best of you, look at it through binoculars but keep your distance—at least for the time being. When co-workers say things like "Plain as the nose on her face" or "I can see by the hair on her double chinny chin chin," they aren't necessarily referring to you. AND your cat is going to be getting a urinary infection on the 23rd. The total vet bill will both emotionally and financially bankrupt you, and on the 24th *you* will develop hairball yourself. Well

Virgo, if shit didn't happen I wouldn't have a column. Life can't always be lace and pretty flowers. Give kitty a big hug for Agatha.

Libra *(September 23–October 22)*

Time is so precious to you. Especially when it comes to family and friends. You'll get a sense this month that there just aren't enough hours in a day. Once again you'll be wrong. There are still twenty-four and that is plenty. For your own safety and well-being, take my advice and leave it alone. It works. Screwing around with *time* is not wise. It may well be precious but it's extremely dangerous. Remember what Groucho Marx said: "Time flies like an arrow... Fruit flies like a banana." See what I mean? Anything that flies like an arrow you don't want to annoy by poking at it with a stick. For sake of argument, let's say you *were* able to successfully squeeze just two more hours into a day, bringing it up to a total of twenty-six. At half-time you would introduce into the equation a little irreversible nightmare known as thirteen o'clock. Is this a cage you want to be rattling? Remember what happened to Hickory Dickory Dock. Poor little mouse never knew what hit him. He's just sittin' there one day, knee deep in cheddar and then... "Oh I think I'll climb up that old clock over there." As the story goes, the clock struck one, and the rest got away with minor injuries. Hickory never squeaked again. You've got yourself one dead mouse and a whole lotta bad luck which could have easily been avoided.

Scorpio *(October 23–November 21)*

Oversexed and drooling profusely, you move out into the quagmire of uncertainty we call love. You're dripping on yourself, Scorpio. For heaven's sake, people are beginning to take notice and for all the wrong reasons. Your libido is working for minimum wage. Your self-respect went to the ladies room and never came back. Perhaps you should plunge your stinger into someone who is a little more financially set. The style of music dictates the dance and, unless you fancy doing the horizontal mambo with a

pauper for the next thirty years (if you're extremely unlucky), may I suggest steppin' on out and movin' on up—it's time to get your piece of the pie.

Sagittarius
(November 22–December 21)

Okay Sagittarius, you *are* laughable. So where's your sense of humor? Do you stay at home alone and mope around the house, or kick some ass and start with the one you've been sitting on? Be adventurous. Become a kept lady. If you aren't a little more sociable you will get very eccentric and turn into a bag lady. For your information there is a big difference between a bag lady and a kept lady. A kept lady gets pampered, not to mention a fabulous tan—which is paramount in life. A bag lady *gets bags* and arranges them in some kind of bizarre order, no doubt for some very legitimate reasons. Does this way of life appeal to you? Do you choose a life of scorn over the lap of luxury? I didn't think so.

Capricorn *(December 22–January 19)*

Hey, Capricorn! Around the 13th don't rule out self-sabotage as a form of entertainment. You know all the right buttons to push and you don't even have to go out. You feed on negativity and innuendo. The average serving of negativity contains zero (0.0) grams of fat and is a recognized method of burning calories. And about all you can get from innuendo is a fat lip. But what are you gonna do—punch yourself in the head? No! If life is beginning to seem repetitious, check your stereo; maybe it's just your CD skipping. And, oh yes, in case you were wondering what that big noise was, it's the universe unfolding as it should. Do not try to stop it. It is meant to be. So it unfolds—who cares? Put your nose in something that large when it's trying to unwind and you're going to lose it. Venus, the planet of love, is in Aquarius this month and there isn't a hell of a lot Aquarius can do about it. And if I were *you*, Capricorn, I'd keep my nose out of Aquarius's business—she's carrying a lot of excess fluid this month. But if you want a big jug of water in the face, then by all means keep bothering her.

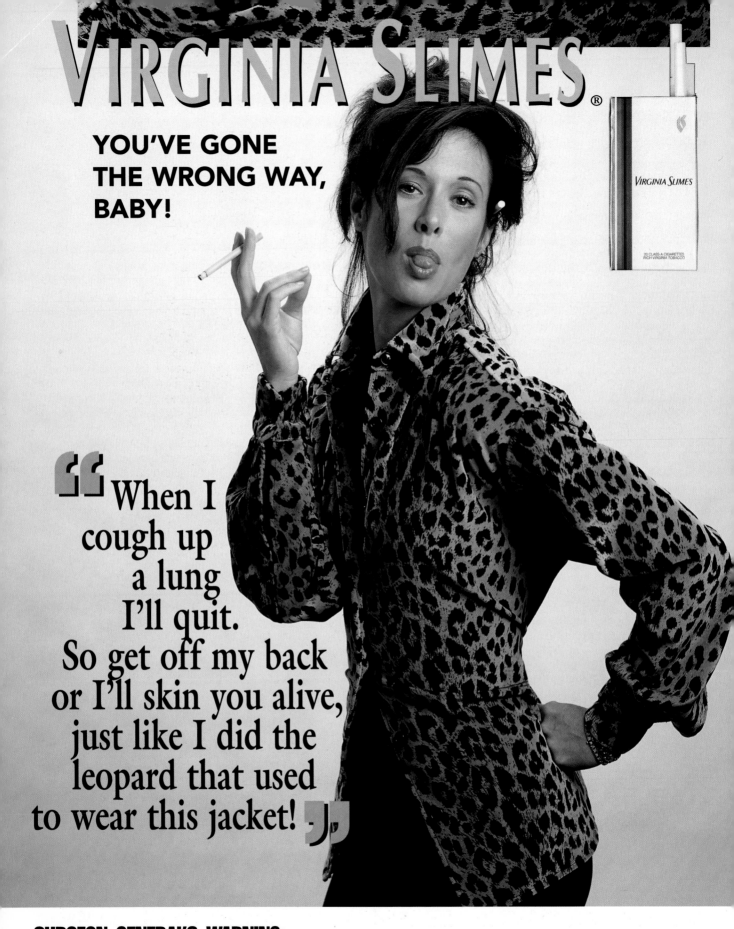

VIRGINIA SLIMES®

YOU'VE GONE THE WRONG WAY, BABY!

VIRGINIA SLIMES

"When I cough up a lung I'll quit. So get off my back or I'll skin you alive, just like I did the leopard that used to wear this jacket!"

"I Buy The Kind That *He* Likes!"

As crazy as it may sound, when we shop for feminine protection "I buy the kind that he likes." Maybe it's a nineties thing, but when it comes to items of a feminine nature, my man knows his stuff. He believes that Happy Liners with panels, channels and now new eaves troughs give me maximum protection with minimal worry. And why wouldn't they? After all, they *were* developed by a woman gynecologist with an Engineering degree.

Happy Liners, "the kind that he likes... and now, thank heavens, I like 'em too."

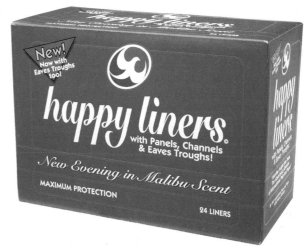

Happy Liners ®

New *Evening in Malibu* scent

From Global Pulp & Paper... Industry in search of the right time of the month.

Vague expectations
Jackie Oh!

The Queen of Camelot or First Lady of Denial?

*t*here was a time in this great land when disposable diapers and aerosol-spray-cheese products could not be bought for love or money; a time when America felt wealthy, powerful and only slightly overweight. The sleek American filter cigarette had all but eliminated cancer, and victory in Vietnam seemed a step away. It was a time that will be remembered for as long as Americans continue to live, breathe, and rent the *JFK* video—a magical era known as Camelot.

> Please don't let it be forgot
> There was a place, or so I thought
> For a brief and shining moment
> A place called Camelot

These were the glory days of John Fitzgerald Kennedy and his beautiful wife Jacqueline Lee Bouvier Kennedy. J.F.K. was young, handsome, charismatic, and according to the mountain of rumor, innuendo and gossip, quite possibly the horniest president in American history. She was graceful and beautiful, with a good designer and a fabulous collection of hats. She knew exactly which side of the butter her toast was stuck to, and she was sticking to it.

It was a special time, a magical time. America once again had a king and queen as they did in 1775 shortly before informing the British of some interesting places to stick their entire sprawling empire. But, much to the horror and disappointment of the American people, Camelot ended tragically on November 22, 1963, when an assassin's bullet smashed through history, killing the president and ruining Jackie's outfit.

Jack and Jackie's happiness was always a little suspect. This soon became painfully obvious when her interests switched from US embargos to Greek shipping, and she married billionaire Aristotle Onassis. Another brilliant Jackie move. She instantly became one of the wealthiest, most famous women in the world—with an even larger collection of fabulous hats.

In 1996, at the request of the children, Camelot went up on the auction block, sold to the highest bidders in the garage sale of the century attended by the rich, famous and surgically altered. It was a star-studded "who's whom," presided over by world renowned Smotherby's Auction House of New York. The event was a smashing success beyond compare. It appeared as though America had lost its marbles but had cleverly brought along their checkbooks to compensate.

Mesmerized by the auctioneer's gavel and hypnotic tone, the bidders took the gloves off in the first round... "All right, ladies and gentlemen, who's gonna bidda bundle for a little bidda Camelot? Do I hear $1 million?... Yeeeeeeeees! Now two mill—gimme two!... Hummina heymina hummina heymina hummina hummina heymina—SOLD!"

ABOVE
Brooch with fake purple stone
(purchased for $1.29, estimated auction price $140,000)

Lite-up plastic roses and vase
(purchased for $16, estimated auction price $1.2 million)

Fake pearls
(from Value Village, $7.95, estimated auction price $350,000)

Jackie hat (opposite page)
(Purchased for $230,
estimated auction price
$2.5 million)

**Opera glasses allegedly
used once by JFK**
(Purchased for$89,
estimated auction price
$275,000)

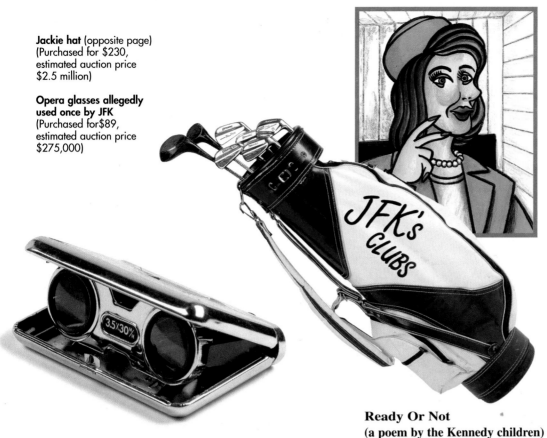

**Fake Picasso
*Pink Pillbox Painting***
(Purchased for $275,
estimated auction price
$6.5 million)

JFK's other set of golf clubs
(Purchased for $425,
estimated auction price
$1.9 million)

**JFK's toothbrush from the
Kennedy Compound**
(Purchased for $3.98,
estimated auction price
$800,000)

**Jackie cover girl
magazines actually
thumbed through
by Jackie**
(Purchased for $1.50 each,
estimated auction
price $25,000 each)

No one was more surprised and delighted than the Kennedy children: J.F.K. Jr. (who has found his niche in publishing, a respectable career which puts distance between him and the words "oversexed pretty-boy playboy socialite bar-exam-failing brat"), and Caroline Kennedy Schlossburger, now an author whose works include *My Own Private Privacy, My Summers at the Kennedy Compound* and her latest best-selling title, *Beyond Hamburger Helper—A book about what to do with ground beef to ensure that it doesn't go bad in the fridge.*

Now Smotherby's has announced, at the request of the children—again!—that there are more boxes of stuff and rumors of even *more* boxes of stuff. This collection covers Jackie's pack-rat and garage sale era and will be offered up to the Camelot-hungry public who missed out on the first round of consignments.

Ready Or Not
(a poem by the Kennedy children)

Ready or not it must be bought
No waffling 'round the golden spot
Give us your bid or you'll get *naught*
No bid, no piece of Camelot.
The end is near and it's all we've got
Till we find some more of Camelot.
All sales final!!!!!

Jacqueline Lee Bouvier Kennedy Onassis. The name suggests that, well, here is someone who's met a few people. Given a bit more time her name could have been much longer.

These pages feature a sampling of the catalog items consigned in Smotherby's up-and-coming estate sale; *Jackie O, The Garage Sale Years.* Smotherby's has very thoughtfully shown the original purchase price along with estimated auction selling price.

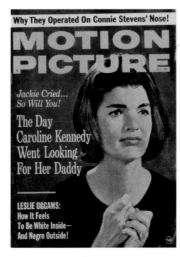

"Kennedy kids sell off *more* Jackie O. stuff."

Sucks fat 'cause fat sucks.

Lypo King®
HOME LIPOSUCTION UNIT

Eduardo Rodriguez Exxon Valdez

WORLD CHAMPION
Dr. Eduardo Rodriguez Exxon Valdez,
winner of Scalpelmania and inventor of the world's first
Home Liposuction Unit. It's available in over 86 countries, at
grocery and hardware chains. Look for it beside the
do-it-yourself carpet-cleaning and Wet-Vac displays.

Overwhelming discomfort in the comfort of your own home.

WARNING: home liposuction may not be suitable for everyone.
Please consult a physician or a carpet-cleaning specialist in your area before renting.

When nature calls...

When you've gotta go, you've gotta go.

Nothing should ever stand between you and your goal, no matter what it is!

Now, with the revolutionary new design of Easy Access Pantyhose, nothing ever does.

Easy Access Pantyhose
The one with the door ®

© L'access de Simple. Une division de Pantyhose de Paris.

broken home furnishings
For better *and* for worse

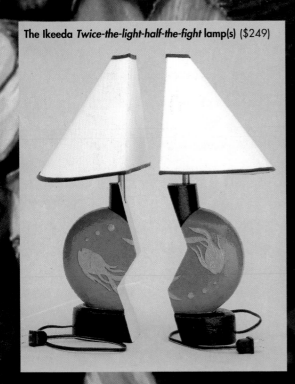

The Ikeeda *Twice-the-light-half-the-fight* lamp(s) ($249)

Should you decide to carve things up the old-fashioned way, why not try out these accessories, which are also from Sweden.
Helmet with protective visor ($85)
T-shirt ($42)
Shorts ($65)
Husquavarna Big Orange gum boots ($125)
Husquavarna chain saw ($524)

Breaking up used to be a dusty, dirty, embarrassing job…large items had to be taken out onto the front lawn to be sawed in half.

The Ikeeda *Breakin' Up Ain't Hard to Do* table(s) ($695)

Divorce-proof furniture with a split personality.

The Ikeeda *Take It AND Leave It* leather couch(es) ($1400)

Now when he says "I want half the couch!" let him have it.

t he gambling spirit is dead. Nobody flips a coin for anything anymore. With marriage breakups on the rise and the mathematics of splitting things fairly becoming more difficult, *Ikeeda*, the Swedish furniture crafters, has created a line which appears to have taken the word unreasonable out of the divorce equation.

Breaking up used to be a dusty, dirty, embarrassing job. We all know the routine: small articles are treated like priceless treasures; large items are taken out onto the front lawn to be sawed in half. Tempers rage, chain saws drone, family pets dive for cover. Neighbors invent outdoor activities in order to secure a legitimate ringside seat. And over in the bushes, a CNN news team waits for the snapping of tempers, that deadly tug-of-war over a pair of polyester pants... Ahh!! The 15 minutes of fame you never wanted in the first place.

All this humiliation will soon be brought to an end by Ikeeda's new line of furniture, fresh off the boat from Sweden (the country that took sex out of the bedroom and placed it back where it belongs—in the middle of the kitchen floor). Now, when he announces that he wants half the couch, he can have it!

Ikeeda did its initial test-marketing on home turf. After the furniture's introduction to the Swedish market, research workers observed that family violence dropped by half and sales doubled immediately following a breakup. It's a boon for the economy and a win for human relations!

At present Ikeeda is test-marketing a couch, a lamp and a coffee table in twenty-one countries. If the results prove positive, it will begin marketing a full line of split-decision Broken Home Furnishings®. Ikeeda is also negotiating a joint venture with Volvo involving an eight-wheeled dissectible automobile and big plans to take the divorce show on the road.

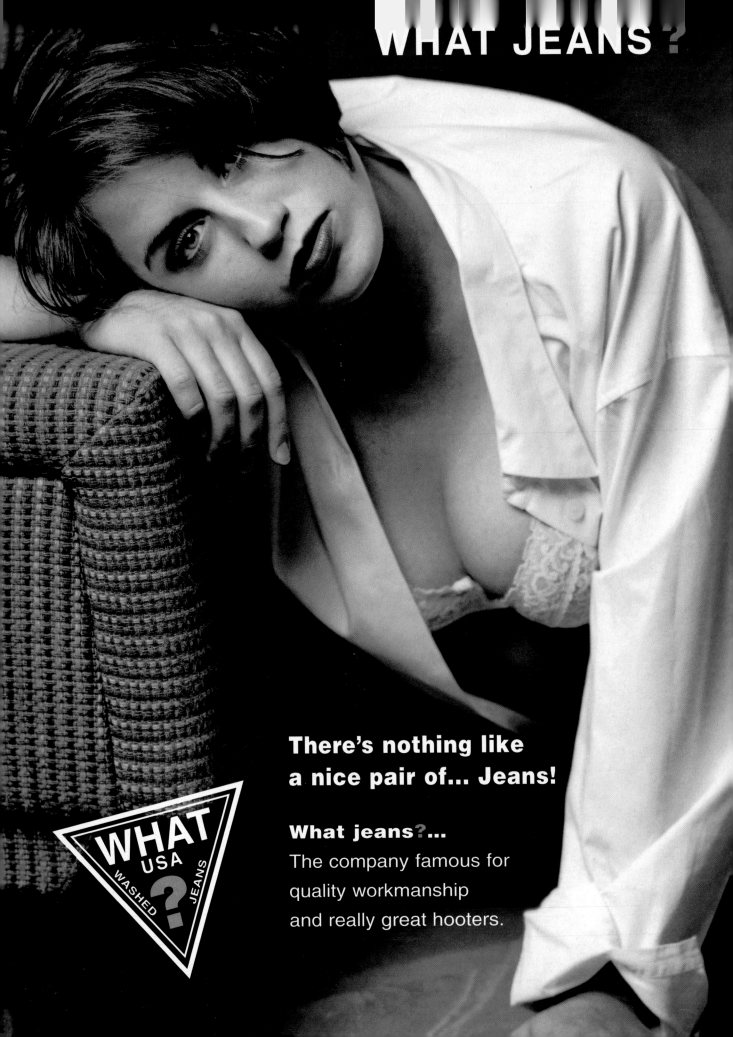

In an Ocean of Competition, Benelton Chooses Shock Images and Controversy to Increase Public Awareness

ROME – Oliverto Toscanio is the man responsible for Benelton's infamous advertising campaigns. He maintains, "If an ad doesn't stir controversy it is mediocre at best."

Toscanio creates controversial ad themes ,but not just to increase sales. In fact, he's not even sure if sales have improved. He claims their purpose is to communicate the message that Benelton is a global company with deep concerns about "society as a hole."

His awareness-raising campaigns depicting animals copulating, naked bodies tattooed H.I.V. POSITIVE, blood-drenched Bosnian soldiers, and an Asian version of the Pope, to name a few, have both angered and delighted customers.

It all began when Toscanio was fourteen. His father took him to a soccer match and left him there. He gave him a camera and ten dollars. Six hours later he came back to pick him up. On the way home in the car he asked, "So, my son, did you learn anything today worthy of my interest and praise?" Toscanio replied, "Yes father, I did. I learned that Italian women will pose naked for almost anyone—even for fourteen-year-old boys—especially when their jibber jabber jibber jabber husbands are more interested in a bunch of sweat-drenched hairy-legged men

kicking a ball around than they are with female companionship... And they're willing to pay top dollar for the experience."

After arriving home his father discovered that young Oliverto now had three hundred dollars and six rolls of film of naked women. His father realized there and then that his son had already developed what it takes to make it in the world of arts and advertising.

Realizing that the exposure to nudity had probably sparked his son's creative vision, Toscanio's father quickly removed Oliverto's clothes and enrolled him in an arts school for the extremely twisted but gifted. He also bought him his own camera equipment and promised to take him to soccer games whenever the home team was playing.

Toscanio credits his father for getting him on track at such a tender age. As both an art director and photographer, he has been responsible for the advertising campaigns of many international firms, including *Esprit Jeans* and *Club Med*. He has also worked for *Elle*, *Vague* and *Harper's Bizarre* magazines.

He has been accused by his critics of image terrorism, of exploiting humanity and suffering to sell a few t-shirts. Such attacks do not bother him, and no subject is too

taboo. He even picks fault with God, saying that "There are so many imperfections in creation that God, shouldn't have taken a rest on the seventh day." The only thing that upsets him is that he won't be able to photograph the moment of his own death. He jokingly quips, "Unless they allow cameras in hell!"

Toscanio must be doing something right. Each year Benelton reportedly sells 80 million garments worldwide. THE UNITED MONEY BAGS OF BENELTON? Undoubtedly, yes!

He may well be an artist and a legend in his own mind, but for those of you who mistrust advertising, his immediate responsibility is to his employer—which means integrity will ultimately take a backseat to making the cash register ring.

Toscanio was surprised by the negative reaction from women's groups over this ad. He claims that the concept represents third-world prostitution, as well as the choke-hold big business has on women.

Leash with an option to buy.

UNITED COLLARS OF BENELTON.

The Incredible Fear Of Average

According to a new study published by the New England Journal of Unusual Studies, the average woman today feels modestly average or slightly below average at best. This is not surprising considering that the law of "above average" seems to be determined by how large your breasts are, how taut your buttocks have become and how incredibly well you've preserved yourself.

It isn't even partly consoling to know that Pamela Anderson's tits are not real. Women don't care. They seem to want them and that's it. We're living in an age where the odds of achieving virtual happiness without first spending a fortune on renovations are not good. The average woman simply hasn't got the financial resources—the deck is heavily stacked against her. The virtual impossibilities of a few short years ago are, well, virtual realities today. But in this age of cyberspace and virtual realness it is disturbing to discover that nobody even cares

that real isn't real anymore. Women want a reasonable facsimile of Pamela's breasts, and most men want to invent a national contact sport centered around them. Theme park designers are ready, poised and standing by to add their own personal touch and twist to the subject on the long shot that there is a radical shift in moral values. If there is even a remote possibility of making millions by building an adult amusement park based on Pamela Anderson's amazon physique then it shall surely come to pass... and pass it will, into obscurity, almost as quickly as will Pamela herself.

> "It isn't even partly consoling to know that Pamela Anderson's boobs are not real. Women don't care. They seem to want them and that's it."

Editorial cartoon from *Travel and Pleasure* magazine showing men storming the front gates on opening day at Pam-A-Land Amazon Theme Park in southern California.

Condom Loses Maternity Clinic
IS THERE AN OBSTETRICIAN IN THE HOUSE?

It appears as though it's too little too late for Condom, a town in southwestern France. Since 1994 condoms have been made available at no charge to the 7000 residents—and the effect of the campaign has taken its toll. Births have dropped, and all the gynecologists have moved out of town. Without a gynecologist, the maternity clinic will be forced to close. Like a meat shop without a butcher, the clinic will cease to be. Although the town has in essence been practicing extremely safe sex, you can't help but wonder if sex can be too safe.

The chamber of commerce has recommended putting a lid on the free condom campaign to see if practicing safe sex in moderation will make a difference.

Condom, near Bordeaux, does a booming business in postcards each year because of its name. The town's name comes from the medieval Condo-magos, meaning "the crossroads of the market."

If you're a gynecologist and would like to know the women of Condom more intimately (which may be why you entered the profession in the first place), give city hall a call. They've got an office with your name on the door waiting for you.